THE SCIENCE AND SPIRIT OF

MANAGEMENT

ANDRÉ FAIZI ALVES

Verba Publications
Copyright © 2014 André Faizi Alves

1st Edition
ISBN-13: 978-0-9892690-0-1
Library of Congress Cataloging-in-Publication Data

Main Editor: Terry Fravel
Assistant Editor: Stephanie Alves
Proofreader: Nancy Markovich
Cover design by Irfan Kokabi
Graphics and tables created by the author, unless credited otherwise.

Wholesale ordering information:
wholesale@TheScienceAndSpiritOfManagement.com

For our course visit:
www.TheScienceAndSpiritOfManagement/Course

Printed by CreateSpace

Dedicated to managers who strive for excellence—of whom Dimas R. Martins Jr. is a fine example.

Acknowledgment

Infinite gratitude to Ms. Terry Fravel, Ms. Nancy Markovich, and my wife Stephanie for their incredible work in bringing this author's English closer to that of native speakers. Although the idiomatic gap has not been completely closed, it is hoped that the ideas contained in this book will compensate for any remaining disparities between my first language and English.

André Faizi

Contents

Preface

The Science and Spirit of Management is the result of unique life experiences that combine an extremely diversified professional career, academic studies, research, exposure to spiritual teachings, lectures—especially in the areas of Organization Development and Organization & Methods—and, above all, much reflection.

The origin of this book can be traced to coaching efforts that spanned more than a decade throughout different organizations and industries in different countries. It evolved to become very successful training material, until it was eventually developed into book format. The final product is a comprehensive, yet concise, survey of management knowledge that makes significant contributions to any manager's performance, regardless of the stage in his or her career.

Initially, the material for this book was geared towards managers lacking significant exposure to management theory. However, based on a new paradigm that reconciles human nature with the true purpose of organizations, it has evolved to contain a coherent explanation of what management is and what managers are supposed to do. For this reason, it can certainly be of benefit to all, from aspiring or new, to even seasoned managers.

The benefits for managers who master management theory can be compared to those of musicians who learn music theory.

To begin with, most people who are not musicians experience music as a whole. That is, people in this category can hardly, if at all, identify notes, scales, chords, tempo, melody, harmony, and so on. Then there are those who learn to play music by ear, or by rote. Still, without the knowledge of music theory, musicians who learn to play only by ear have a hard time producing anything new. Their learning is achieved mostly by copying others, which means that they tend to incorporate, without distinction, both the strengths and weaknesses of those whom they copy. Theory provides the mechanism for facilitating the development and transposition of ideas from the abstract into the concrete world. It allows for freedom and for advancement.

The same happens to most individuals in management. The goal here is to assist managers to learn theory and develop the skills that will allow them to see beyond the whole and move past "management by rote".

Managers should not get used to carrying out their duties simply by:

- *Copying best practices* – For example, departmentalization is a concept that can be easily overlooked because managers often feel quite comfortable with how to organize work in their area of expertise. Ironically, when organizations need help, consultants that are brought in very often dedicate a considerable portion of their efforts to re-departmentalizing and restructuring the organization.

- *Relying on the synergy created by all members in the organization* – Despite bad management, synergy can help many organizations survive longer than one would expect. Regardless of synergy, if an organization is to prosper, proper management eventually becomes necessary.

Anyone who is serious about being a manager should dedicate some time to reading and studying at least a few books that explore basic management concepts. It is essential for individuals to have solid intellectual foundations, so that they can be empowered to achieve excellence in their endeavors, and thus better contribute to society.

Introduction

The Science and Spirit of Management approaches the subject of management through the new paradigm of the oneness of humanity. This paradigm facilitates the explanation of the role of management in the formation and functioning of organizations as organic systems truly harmonized with the concept of human beings as social and spiritual beings.

Contrary to what one might think, the questions *What is management?* and *What are managers supposed to do?* have indeed been difficult to answer, even though the subject of management has been a concern for centuries.

Notwithstanding such difficulty, outstanding contributions were made in particular by the group of thinkers that constituted the Classical School of Management[1], with special distinction to Henri Fayol (1841 – 1925).

Unfortunately, instead of building on previous contributions, generations since the Classical School have chosen a path for developing the discipline that has made the concept of management and the functions of a manager more elusive than what they once were.

Evidence of this lack of clarity can be inferred from the following:

- Current variations in the definition[2] of what management is and in the explanations of what managers are supposed to do

- The lack of standardization in the use of many key terminologies fundamental to the understanding of the discipline of management, like roles, traits, styles, techniques, methods, departmentalization, and delegation

- The familiar criticism against educational institutions that expresses dissatisfaction with their ability to prepare their students to adequately serve as managers

- The common practice of promoting people to their first managerial positions based primarily on their non-managerial knowledge

- The desire of many to replace managers with leaders

At least three factors are at the root of this difficulty in clarifying the subject of management:

1. The disproportional focus on the need for acquiring non-managerial knowledge of specialized areas in detriment of learning the underlying principles that govern the discipline

2. The abstract notion of boundaries articulated through the idea of management levels, and the dynamics between them. The fact is that management functions are in essence the same at all levels, although they receive differentiated attention and their characteristics vary some, depending on the level

3. The embracing of a concept of human nature that leads to a misalignment with the true purpose of organizations—that is, the acceptance of the belief that individual profit can supersede social wellbeing

Thus, this book approaches the subject of management with the notion that a manager is one of many components that must work in harmony to allow for the existence of healthy organizations. This means that although his or her work needs to be carried out from distinctive hierarchical positions in the organizational structure, this does not excuse managers from an "ethic of reciprocity and balance" called for by the principle of "unity in diversity".

> *A sustainable social order is distinguished, among other things, by an ethic of reciprocity and balance at all levels of human organization. A relevant analogy is the human body: here, millions of cells collaborate to make human life possible. The astounding diversity of form and function connects them in a lifelong process of giving and receiving. It*

represents the highest expression of unity in diversity. Within such an order, the concept of justice is embodied in the recognition that the interests of the individual and of the wider community are inextricably linked. The pursuit of justice within the frame of unity (in diversity) provides a guide for collective deliberation and decision-making and offers a means by which unified thought and action can be achieved.[3]

Bahá'í International Community

This book is divided into three parts as follows:

Part I – FOUNDATION

Part I draws attention to two key components in the framework of the discipline of management, namely Human Beings and Organizations. The importance of exploring these components rests on the fact that, depending on how they are conceptualized, the understanding and practice of the discipline of management take on significantly distinct directions. Additionally, Part I identifies work domains where managers can, and in some instances must, operate. Altogether, the above knowledge should raise awareness of and better prepare managers to deal with a number of aspects of their work that tend to go unidentified during day-to-day operations.

Part II – MANAGING

Part II delves into management itself, exploring the concept and functions of management, its span of direct responsibility, managers' personal qualities and approaches, and different ways to implement shared management.

Part III – SUPPLEMENT

Because the realm of management knowledge is vast, Part III presents popular topics under the classifications of Management Tools, Management Programs, and Managers' Functional Areas of Expertise, to assist managers to gain better footing in the discipline of management.

PART I

Foundation

1

Human Beings

Clearly, in order to explore any subject, the concept of a human being deserves profound consideration. However, it is of paramount importance in management, because, consciously or unconsciously, it guides all aspects of a manager's work. Since such an undertaking can easily reach colossal proportions and divert the focus from the central theme of this book, only a few vital points related to this topic are addressed here.

In the interest of simplification, the existing concepts about human reality might be arranged into two paradigms.

1. One paradigm considers humans nothing more than animals, something akin to apes. The difference between other animals and humans is that so far only humans have managed to undergo key biological adaptations that have catapulted our species into major breakthroughs, especially in the area of brain development. In this case, the purpose of life is to satisfy physical and psychological needs. This construct sees humans as slaves to the same natural laws that govern the animal kingdom, such as competition, survival of

the fittest, dominion over geographical territories, and an unrestrained manifestation of all physical impulses.

2. The other paradigm considers humans spiritual beings. This paradigm recognizes that the animal kingdom possesses the qualities of growth and reproduction existent in the lower vegetable kingdom, plus the quality of the senses. In turn, humans possess the qualities of the two previous kingdoms and a third characteristic, referred to as the soul[1]. In this scenario, the life of the spirit, or the rational soul, which is not material, does not end with the destruction of the physical body[2]. Therefore, one of the main purposes of the time spent on this planet is the acquisition of spiritual qualities such as love, justice, truthfulness, honesty, trustworthiness, compassion, and patience, which are necessary for a life of plenitude in the next world.

Furthermore, essential to the understanding of human reality is the topic of free will[3]. This power, which (according to the second paradigm described above) is not present in other beings, endows humans with the capacity to make decisions, allowing them to go against physical, social, and spiritual laws. For instance, even though humans are by nature social beings, unlike any other species that also depends on social composition for survival, we have often exploited our own kin, thus acting contrary to the basic principle of cooperation that should govern our organizations. Another significant case in point is our power of free will that allows us to poison or even to kill ourselves intentionally, going against the instinct of self-preservation.

Compounding the complexity of exercising our free will is the fact that the consequences of disrespecting spiritual, social, and even physical laws are not always clear. These become even less clear as our focus moves from physical to social laws, and from social to spiritual laws. For example, the consequence of disrespecting the law of gravity is very clear. Just consider the result of jumping from the top of a high-rise, instead of using an elevator or stairs. In contrast, the consequences of disrespecting social laws can be less evident. By driving through a red traffic light one might get into an accident, get a ticket, or pass through without any apparent negative outcome. In turn, consequences of disrespecting spiritual laws, such as justice, might not be at all understood and, therefore, be completely ignored. Even more difficult to see are the consequences that a lack of respect of a law in one reality has on other realities.

Thus, a clear awareness of a concept of human beings is necessary for managers to better align their thoughts and actions with theories and operations. Moreover, the implementation of such a proposition requires attention to a negative consequence of the over-application of the departmentalization formula—that is, the false notion that it is possible to segregate one's life into disconnected areas. Family, professional, religious, political and social lives are some of the areas that many try to departmentalize. As a result, it is common to find people who profess adherence to one belief but are inconsistent through different settings, for example loving one another at church, but adopting wild animal principles in the business world.

> *It's not what you know that gets you in trouble. It's what you know that ain't so.*
>
> Author unknown

2

Organizations

Like the concept of human beings, the concept of organizations, which is an offshoot of the former, is of fundamental importance to a manager's performance. After all, it is in the organizational context that managers exist. Still, many managers are used to walking into their organizations every day without ever thinking about how aligned the organization is with its true reality. This awareness is important, because—in the same way that our free will allows us to go against nature—it allows us to go against the organization's true purpose.

> Granted that efficiency is essential in everything that is worth the doing, we must not forget that efficiency is never an end in itself. It must always have an aim and purpose and it can only justify itself through the worthiness of this purpose. Worthiness in the industrial sphere can have reference to one thing only, namely the contribution of industry to the sum total of human welfare. On this basis only must industry and all its works finally be judged.[1]
>
> James D. Mooney

The concept of an organization as *an association of people laboring towards a common purpose* is fine, but it is possible and beneficial to deepen our understanding of this concept.

The problem with the above definition of an organization is that it has given many of us an opportunity to forget the *common purpose* part of the characterization and instead turn our focus to the *association of people*, subsequently narrowing it down to an emphasis on the interest of a few or of each individual.

Now, if we approach organizations as single entities or units, the way we often do with the concept of teams, managers' decisions will surely accommodate the needs and inputs of all involved. At the same time, isolated interests that run contrary to a group's interests become unacceptable[2].

Under which concept can internal competition exist? In which one are the chances for cooperation more likely? In the first definition of organizations as associations of people, due to the connotation of multiplicity, there is room for individual agendas, need for negotiations, conflict, and lots of wasted energy. In other words, when the focus is shifted to individuals, conditions for internal competition are created.

With the concept of an organization as a single unit, counterproductive issues fade away. The interests of the individuals and those of the organizations—that is, of the parts and that of the whole—become naturally harmonized. Moreover, the potential of both individuals and of the group can be manifested to their fullest. In this mode of operation—the group, the unit does not compete with itself.

The elaboration of the Bahá'í International Community on Bahá'u'lláh's analogy, which compares society to the human body, presents precisely the idea that we are trying to convey:

> *Human society is composed not of a mass of merely differentiated cells but of associations of individuals, each one of whom is endowed with intelligence and will; nevertheless, the modes of operation that characterize man's biological nature illustrate fundamental principles of existence. Chief among these is that of unity in diversity. Paradoxically, it is precisely the wholeness and complexity of the order constituting the human body—and the perfect integration into it of the body's cells—that permit the full realization of the distinctive capacities inherent in each of these component elements. No cell lives apart from the body, whether*

in contributing to its functioning or in deriving its share from the well-being of the whole. The physical well-being thus achieved finds its purpose in making possible the expression of human consciousness; that is to say, the purpose of biological development transcends the mere existence of the body and its parts.

What is true of the life of the individual has its parallels in human society. The human species is an organic whole, the leading edge of the evolutionary process. That human consciousness necessarily operates through an infinite diversity of individual minds and motivations detracts in no way from its essential unity.[3]

Bahá'í International Community

Additionally,

Since the body of humankind is one and indivisible, each member of the race is born into the world as a trust of the whole, this trusteeship constitutes the moral foundation of most of the other rights—principally economic and social...[4]

Bahá'í International Community

2.1 *Organizational Traits*

Every organization has its own unique traits. Additionally, each organization has traits that are typical to a particular industry.

Managers can be more effective if they are aware of and understand at least some of the key traits that define the organization in which they work and the implications of those traits on their work.

Unfortunately, because managers often join organizations with most of the organization's key traits predetermined, if not already in place, they tend to take such traits for granted and not think about them. For example, for years the great majority of managers of not-for-profit organizations ignored the possibility that their institutions could become self-sufficient.

In addition to managers being conscious of their organizations' traits and understanding how these affect their work, they can also alter the traits themselves, as long as the traits are not the result of governmental laws. For instance:

- Managers can formalize key processes in small organizations, just as formal processes are a strong trait of large institutions.

- Managers can involve their direct reports in the decision-making process of privately-owned organizations, even though in such institutions one of the main traits is centralized decision-making.

Thus, even though key traits provide managers with a framework that tends to affect their decision-making process, they can make wise adaptations that eventually might even run contrary to traits that are perceived as unalterable.

As such, managers must develop the skills necessary to identify and interpret ordinary traits, as well as to be able to uncover new ones specific to their organizations. In this effort, it might be helpful for managers to look for prevailing traits used to classify organizations into different types.

Some classifications are:

Proprietorship

- *Private* – A restricted number of people hold control over the organization's capital.

- *Public* – Shares of the organization are publicly traded. In terms of relationship between capital and labor, this type is similar to Private.

- *Cooperative* – The organization's capital is collectively owned by all internally associated with the enterprise.

- *Governmental* – The organization belongs to a geopolitical society.

Financial Objective

- *For-profit* – The accumulation of wealth by the organization's shareholders is the basic, and in many instances the only, reason for its existence.

- *Not-for-profit* – Promotion of the wellbeing of others, rather than personal gratification, is the main purpose for the organization's existence. Provisions, including financial, are seen as a "means" to achieve objectives and not as an "end" in themselves. Nevertheless, not-for-profit organizations must also be economically viable.

Mode of Survival

- *Self-sustaining* – The objective is survival by receiving financial compensation from customers or third parties in exchange for services and goods.

- *Dependent on third party benefactors* – The objective is to provide assistance (services and/or goods) free of charge. In this case, the organization requires financial contributions from third parties to operate.

Deliverable

- *Services*
- *Goods*

Size

- *Micro*
- *Small*
- *Mid-size*
- *Large*
- *Multinational*

Presence

- *Local*
- *Regional*
- *National*
- *Transnational*
- *Global*

Output Quantities

- *Unit*
- *Small lots*
- *Large batches*
- *Mass quantities*

The following table presents a list of core competencies[5] that, when developed by organizations, become organizational traits. It shows how a given trait affects management's operational focus.

Influence of Trait on Management's Operational Focus

Trait (Core Competency)	Objective	Operational Focus
Customer Intimacy	To deliver solutions to customers' needs	Marketing – relationship with customer
Operational Excellence	To deliver at the best prices with ease	Operations – processes efficiency, cost reduction
Product Leadership	To deliver better and cutting-edge products	Research and Development – creativity, innovation

Table 2.1

Further employing the concept of core competencies, another example of the importance of being aware of organizational traits can be found in the pitfall of engaging in Customer Intimacy practices that undercut profitability in organizations that have operational excellence as their core competency.

In summary, through awareness of organizational traits, managers become better prepared to make decisions related to each of their functions, the selection of management programs, and the utilization of tools.

2.2 Organizational Life Cycle

Broadly speaking, like any other temporal phenomenon, organizations go through the phases of birth, growth, maturity, decline and death, and at each stage, a set of different characteristics is predominant.

This awareness of organizational stages is useful for improving an organization's present performance as well as for assisting with the process of planning and managing the transition from one phase to another, or even for reinventing the organization so that it can move from decline toward advancement.

As is the case with the knowledge of key organizational traits, managers' capacity to identify and incorporate the knowledge of stages into their daily work is an additional asset.

By connecting this concept more directly to day-to-day managerial efforts, the awareness of such knowledge can be applied to what managers are supposed to do but, not necessarily, to what the results of aggregated work should be. In other words, this knowledge should be directed towards how each management function is both influenced by and affects the set of predominant characteristics present in each phase of an organization's life cycle[6].

Nevertheless, because the focus of organizational life cycle is on the organization and not on managers, a model based on organizations is first presented as follows:

Model I – Organizational Life Cycle

	Stage I	**Stage II**	**Stage III**	**Stage IV**	**Stage V**
Dominant Issue	Birth	Growth	Maturity	Decline	Death
Popular Strategies	Concentration in a niche	Horizontal and vertical growth	Concentric and conglomerate diversification	Profit strategy followed by retrenchment	Liquidation or bankruptcy
Likely Structure	Entrepreneur-dominated	Functional management emphasized	Decentralization into profit or investment centers	Structural surgery	Dismemberment of structure

Table 2.2.a – *WHEELEN, THOMAS L.; HUNGER, J. DAVID, STRATEGIC MANAGEMENT AND BUSINESS POLICY, 8th Edition, © 2002. Reprinted by permission of Pearson Education, Inc, Upper Saddle River, NJ.*

It is pertinent to observe that Model I is based on a paradigm of organizational growth that will certainly have to be reviewed, especially in the face of the destructive impact that our materialistic society is having on the planet.

Additionally, it is good to keep in mind that it is not possible to cast the experience of all organizations or managers into a single model. This means that no model can provide a "one size fits all" exposition of reality. At best, it can offer a framework. The examples presented here are offered as a starting point for analyzing one's own situation.

The following model elaborates on the organizational life cycle from the perspective of management functions.

Model II – Stages of Management Functions (Life Cycle)

Management Function	Stages of Management Functions		
	Phase I (Early Stage)	Phase II (Maturing Stage)	Phase III (Advanced Stage)
Leadership / Decision-Making	Centralized in top management.	Centralized in top management with some internal assistance. Some guidance via policies.	Centralized or decentralized with internal and external assistance. Guidance through policies.
Planning	Very little planning. Decisions and actions mainly driven by top manager's intuition and knowledge.	Systematic broad planning with some middle management involvement. Functional areas responsible for confined planning. Some overall organizational alignment.	Methodic and holistic (internal and external considerations) planning with assistance from dedicated support staff. High overall organizational alignment.
Organizing	Little organization. Very much guided by the senses.	Reasonable organization mainly based on best practices without clear link to strategy.	Extremely organized, mixture of best practices and customization in line with strategy.
Provisioning	Struggle for survival. Guided mainly by what is possible and not by what is desired.	Mixture of self-sufficient and external financing. Reasonable control over desired provisions.	Self-sufficient. Extreme control over desired provisions.
Coordinating	Mostly reactive. Solving problems as you go.	Main transfers well-established with continuous adjustments.	Basically all processes rigidly established. Changes based on planning.
Monitoring	Very little monitoring. Mainly personal with assistance of some basic financial indicators.	Diversified key monitoring indicators measured against plan.	Multiple and sophisticated (internal and external) monitoring systems.
Supporting	Very little support, if any at all.	Individual managers' initiatives and eventual programs.	Regular formalized organization-wide programs.
Cultural Modeling	Unconsciously affected by top manager's influence.	Some scattered operational measures, but in general unconsciously affected by top management influence.	Consciously and methodically sought and implemented.
Liaising	Often non-existent due to small organization size.	Not consciously sought. Occasional individual managers' initiatives.	(Today) Special attention is given to external stakeholders. Should be formally institutionalized.

Table 2.2.b

2.3 Formal and Informal Organizational Spheres

A popular way to gain insight into the functioning of an organization and how to work effectively in it, is the idea that every organization is an entity made up of two spheres: one formal and the other informal[7]. Perhaps this twofold composition can be looked at as something analogous to the physical and spiritual aspects of human beings.

This concept of formal and informal spheres is frequently portrayed using the model of an iceberg, where the formal sphere is the visible part of an organization above the water and the informal is the less perceptible part under the water.

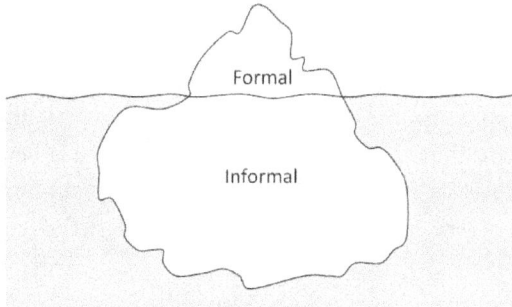

Figure 2.3: Organizational Iceberg

As a version of this model, it follows that:

a) The formal sphere, represented by the tip of the iceberg, is made up of the "non-human" components, such as structure, infrastructure, policies and procedures, technology, services and goods, financial resources, computer software, and brand.

b) The informal sphere, represented by the largest part of the iceberg under water, is made up of the organization's "human" components, like its people and culture. The people component refers to humans' physical, psychological, social, and spiritual needs. Culture here refers to the attitudes, unofficial interactions, combined principles, feelings, perceptions, and so forth, of the people serving in the organization. The dynamics in this sphere have the potential to either assist or undermine the use of individual intelligence and skills, available resources, and management efforts[8].

For our purpose, the most relevant insight that can be gained from this iceberg representation is that, despite its size, the larger informal sphere of the organization generally receives much less attention from managers than the smaller formal sphere.

It is understandably much easier to focus on and therefore act upon what is above water. However, since the informal sphere constitutes the "largest" portion of an organization, managers cannot afford to relegate it to second place. Attention to it requires more than a partial contribution from a function like Supporting. It also necessitates the systematic application of a dedicated management function, like Cultural Modeling.

2.4 Open System and Holistic View

Like everything in creation, organizations do not exist in isolation. They interact with their surroundings, both affecting and being affected by them. In some instances, these interactions are direct, and in others indirect. The recognition of this fact has lead to the articulation of the concept of an organization as an *Open System*[9]. One of the main benefits of this idea is the increasing awareness that organizations cannot be properly managed without regard for external concerns. The same idea is, of course, applicable to individual areas inside the organization.

In time, this concept of an open system has evolved into the notion of a *Holistic View*[10]. In turn, the holist view is consolidating into the notion of a Holistic System, meaning that not only are there connections with external elements, but also everything is interdependent.

Although the need for a holistic approach seems very reasonable, especially in a globalized world, for many people in most situations it is nothing more than a sophisticated, remote concept. That is fine, as the reality of humans as parts of the whole precludes all of us from truly having a holistic view. However, this limitation does not mean that we should not pursue it.

In trying to pursue a holistic approach, the best way is to combine multiple, diverse perspectives[*]. In other words, if one's area of responsibility is not to be managed in isolation from other areas that are internal and external to the organization, one should encourage general participation.

At first, especially at lower levels, some managers might not be able to see much of the impact of external matters on their work. Even so, the list of external considerations that managers have to deal with is numerous indeed, especially as an organization grows in size and/or outreach. Some of

---

[*] This is another very compelling argument in favor of both diversity and teamwork.

the more obvious considerations are supply chain, distribution channels, customer satisfaction, technological changes, government regulations, social responsibility, and equivalent organizations (competitors). In this regard, managers should keep in mind that a holistic approach must go beyond formal issues to include informal ones as well. For example, they can examine how their department is being perceived by other areas in the organization, and how these perceptions are being addressed.

Certainly, the higher the management level, the more relevant a holistic approach becomes. A case in point is the importance and benefit of considering as many factors as reasonably possible during strategic planning, which is a top-level management duty.

To ignore the impact of external matters on an area can be costly indeed. As a result, managers at all levels should incorporate the idea of an open system into their thinking and, as much as possible, approach their work with the principle of a holistic system.

The figure below provides some external elements that should be present in open and holistic thinking:

Figure 2.4: Elements to Consider in Open and Holistic Thinking

2.5 *Departmentalization*

Knowledge of the concepts related to organizations that have been presented so far is not as overt a requirement to management as is the concept of *Departmentalization*[11]. Managers can get by with poor, or in some cases, no awareness of the previous concepts, but without proper attention to the principle of departmentalization, they can easily throw areas under their responsibility into disarray, which might eventually lead to enterprise failure.

Simply put, departmentalization, which is a function of growth, is the endeavor of creating delimited work areas within an organization. This, of course, includes defining the work of even single staff members or single workstations. The final objective of departmentalization is the creation and maintenance of work areas where managers and their direct reports can perform at their best.

To achieve that, managers should cluster work based primarily on the degree of similarity, followed by the level of complementarity, in ways that allow processes to take place. The result is the creation of specialized areas.

The principle that governs the endeavor of departmentalization is analogous to the one that drives the formation of the human body. The human body is the result of the division of cells and their clustering into different specialized groups in order to form organs, members, and so on, which in turn together create the final organism. Organizations, too, have diverse, specialized work areas: individuals with different work assignments, sections, divisions, departments, agencies, branches, and business units.

Regardless of whether or not departmentalization endeavors are planned and institutionalized, or implemented by way of partial or overall redesign, they always develop as a result of the division or addition of work, or a combination of both.

For example:

a. Departmentalization occurs through division when the work of a single work area is divided among two or more existing and/or new work areas. Perhaps the most common reasons for dividing the work of a work area are reaching a workload limit or reaching a low level of correlation between the diverse types of work carried out in the area, either of which can make the initial arrangement counter-productive. In other words, the existing work arrangement starts to negatively affect the performance of an individual, a work area, and/or a manager. Departmentalization through division can also be sought as a proactive measure with the objective of improving the performance of an area.

b. Departmentalization is achieved through addition when new work is added to an area, or when a completely new area of functionality is created. For example, upper management might add a new department of Quality Control or Research & Development where such functionality did not previously exist.

c. Departmentalization occurs through a combination of division and addition, in sequential steps, especially in major redesign interventions. In this case, some of the work that has been divided will form distinct new areas, some will remain in the original area(s) or be eliminated, while other work will be added to other previously existent or new area(s).

The dynamics of departmentalization might sound very simple. However, like cooking, it is not enough to just mix some ingredients and stir over heat for a while. In practice, to achieve a satisfactory result with cooking, the exact selection of ingredients, their quantities, the sequence and timing of the mixture, and the temperature, among other things, are fundamental. It is the same with the implementation of departmentalization. Many factors need to be taken into consideration. It should also be noted that a new arrangement in one area might affect other areas and/or elicit the creation of new ones.

With a background of issues such as organizational traits, organizational life cycle phases, open systems, administrative levels, and formal and informal organizational spheres, some factors that can be taken into consideration when departmentalizing are the following:

- Cost structure
- Customers
- Deliverables
- Geographical arrangement
- In-house versus outsourcing
- Internal control

- Objectives
- Political concerns (not a commendable reason but it does occur)
- Quality of process
- Quantity
- Readiness for change
- Shifts
- Specialization
- Staff qualifications
- Strategy

As a result, there is no single or right way to proceed with departmentalization, and consequently there are no final unique arrangements for work areas. There are, however, arrangements resulting from best practices that can be used as general templates.

Many departmentalization endeavors should be carried out through careful planning. Depending on the complexity of such endeavors, they should also be supported by management programs like Change Management and Project Management.

2.6 *Organizational Structure*

After the departmentalization endeavor has been completed, the work areas must now be assembled together to form a single entity. The arrangement obtained with this all-inclusive assembling is called the *Organizational Structure*[12]. Of course, this description of a very distinct and sequential way of departmentalizing and then structuring can only occur during the creation of an organization or during an overall redesign. More often than not, the clusters resulting from the division and/or addition of work have to be themselves united or clustered with other parts of the organization on a case-by-case basis.

To avoid confusion between the results of departmentalization and organizational structure, it is useful to observe that sometimes the difference is just a matter of point of reference. For instance, a large organization might be the aggregate of different business units which, by themselves, can be seen as independent organizational structures. However, in the context of the larger organization, the business units are nothing more than single work areas. In other words, each area created by departmentalization has its own structure, and the term "organizational structure" is reserved for expressing only the larger, final entity that is formed by the integration of the smaller work areas.

Even though it is common to classify organizational structures into different types, the reality is that almost all organizations have a functional structure as their bedrock. That is, they are based on work specialization. The other classifications are, for the most part, adaptations or appendages to certain functional areas. For example, structures referred to as staff-and-line, collegiate, and teams do not illustrate organizations as a whole; they represent only some specific areas, and are often combined within a functional structure. Matrix and project-based structures represent continual or temporary combinations of a number of functional structures. Unitary, holding, and divisional structures, on the other hand, exhibit only top administrative levels, as they are employed to facilitate the governance of large institutions. Network, virtual, and cellular structures are examples that represent relations between different combinations of areas or structures mentioned above.

It is relevant to notice that whatever shape an organizational structure takes on paper, in practice it will have the shape of a pyramid. Such an organizational pyramid may be more or less flat. It can have a very pointed tip, as is the case with a single top manager, or the tip can be flattened where a committee serves in place of a single individual. Regardless of its variations, the need to observe hierarchy will not tolerate structures with too many generals and too few soldiers, or only generals, or only soldiers.

To achieve an arrangement where the integrating parts form an organic entity, in which all its parts provide for and benefit from each other, the structuring process requires more than merely positioning each work area inside an overall scheme. It must also establish the lines of relationship and the procedures that should connect and govern the hierarchy and work flow of these areas.

The final aim is to create organizational structures that are, overall, both stable and effective for a reasonable period. This, however, should not cause us to shun changes. We must accept that organizations, as organic entities, will necessarily be changing over time. During certain periods, organizations experience little or no perceptible change in their structure, while at other times, they undergo moderate or even major restructuring, whether planned or unplanned.

Having a well-designed structure is so important that major efforts to improve organizations quite often involve re-departmentalization and re-structuring. Consequently, restructuring is not an undertaking that should be embarked upon carelessly. In addition to being potentially costly, re-structuring can have broad and complex implications. Examples include changes in staffing, the redesign of processes, hierarchy modifications, and market repositioning. Especially in medium and large organizations, re-structuring requires considerable expertise for successful implementation.

Since there is no single or right way to departmentalize, there is no single or right way to structure organizations. The most important consideration when doing so should be strategy, as articulated in the saying, "structure follows strategy"[13].

The standard way of graphically describing organizational structures is through the use of organizational charts.

Figure 2.6: Organizational Chart

Example of functional structure with shared management, where managers from each functional area plus a dedicated executive secretary compose an executive committee.

3

Work Domains

A Work Domain is a concept intended to place work into particular spheres or arenas. By classifying work in such a way, managers should have an easier time observing and addressing work in its different formats and contexts.

By observing and understanding particular work domains, many of which usually go unidentified, managers should, for instance, be able to determine which management function or functions, personal management qualities, tools are more relevant to each domain. In short, managers should be able to select the functions that primarily relate to Process, tap into the personal quality that most significantly addresses intrapersonal work, satisfactorily align functional areas to corporate strategy, and adopt rewards and penalties that are conducive to teamwork.

Although many work domains are subtle realities, nevertheless they are very important to a manager's performance. A clear grasp of domains also serves as a strong basis for the conceptualization of many other ideas in the discipline of management. It is hoped that managers will develop the skills and habits to observe and act upon most domains, to the degree that these efforts can make a significant difference in the discharge of their daily duties.

3.1 Intrapersonal Work Domain

For the purpose of this book, the intrapersonal work domain is the abstract, subjective domain where work is carried out at the intellectual level and which should precede all objective work. This means that the quality of our objective work depends on the quality of our thinking.

The idea of an intrapersonal work domain may sound strange to some, but let us not forget that all our affairs, our organizations, our society, and everything that we create in this world are expressions of what is formed in our minds.

For managers, this matter of intrapersonal work has considerable weight, because management positions are among those that have to deal with the highest percentage of subjective work. This being the case, managers should dedicate a considerable portion of their time and energy to thinking.

Reduced dedication to intrapersonal work, which consequently results in an increase of focus on objective work, can cause many managers to fall into the micromanagement trap. Managers who do not take the time to think properly about the execution of their functions could end up basing their management on what they can perceive through the senses.

Of course, different management functions at different administrative levels call for a different amount of dedication to this work domain. In the case of a duty like monitoring simple reoccurring daily physical work, it is understandable that little or no time be dedicated to reflection. However, in the case of other duties like planning strategy, problem-solving complex issues, coordinating sophisticated processes, or even improving the work of monitoring, managers must devote a considerable amount of time to reflection to achieve even satisfactory results.

Often, in situations when reflection is required but instead subjective work is hastily performed, clarity of understanding can hardly be reached. This practice can easily become the source of faulty decision-making, eventually leading to all sorts of problems, such as injustice, misjudgment of priorities, incoherence between activities, and misalignment with strategy.

To ameliorate the situation of those who usually dedicate very little time to this work domain, many organizations are presently set up and run in such a way that there is not much opportunity for managers to reflect. Most organizations are constantly trying to reduce costs by overloading their employees with work, creating unhealthy work environments. Surely, there are also those who are, as a product of a consumer society, just used to taking in information without having developed the habit of processing it.

Work in the intrapersonal domain is exclusively an individual matter. It is not carried out through interaction with others. It must be done unaided, through individual reflection. Some of the work that has been done individually should be examined later and perfected at the group level, using consultation (see section 6.2.2), which is to a group as individual reflection is to a person.

3.2 Interpersonal Work Domain

The interpersonal[1] work domain is the realm of work that exists as a result of human interaction, through either direct or indirect contact. Managers should be most concerned with direct contact, since it is more likely to generate significant results.

In the case of indirect contact, it is much harder to reach the level of closeness that direct contact can create. Because it has less capacity to transmit human emotion, indirect contact can easily be interpreted as cold, distant, indifferent, or unfriendly. Direct or personal contact, on the other hand, has all the ingredients to be more lively, engaging, affable, compassionate, and friendly. In-person contact is the most complete form of communication. It can stimulate the senses to their utmost capacity, facilitating the triggering of feelings, and allowing for immediate feedback of equal intensity to take place. Adversely, direct contact has the potential to be much more unpleasant than indirect contact—so much so that many try to avoid it, for fear of running into contentious, hostile situations.

By allowing for better reading of people and the possibility of comparing their behavior with their words, direct contact also helps to build trust. Direct contact is a fundamental necessity for human beings. In fact, it is a necessity of every creature that depends on social structure for its existence.

As a result, it can strengthen relationships and increase collaboration, which is a sine qua non characteristic of organizations.

That being the case, managers should consider the advantages of physical proximity, which tends to increase the frequency and, with time, the quality of interactions. In many cases, it is easier and faster to talk to someone than to send a message and wait for a reply. Even in the eventuality of an immediate reply from indirect communication, it often cannot address all aspects of the issue at hand in a satisfactory way. Subsequent messages are usually necessary to fill in gaps, answer questions and clarify misunderstandings in order to bring about an acceptable conclusion.

There are major variations in how managers carry out work in this domain. At one extreme of the interpersonal work spectrum, there are those managers who like to use in-person contact as their primary means of interaction with their direct reports, and whenever possible with superiors, peers, clients, and other stakeholders. For these managers, a practical challenge can be in finding an amount of interaction that does not take up too much valuable time. Without a balanced approach regulated by good organization and discipline, a manager's day can easily evaporate.

At the other extreme, we find those managers who prefer to keep in-person contact to a minimum. They prefer indirect forms of communication like written messages, often using a secretary, and, when there is no alternative, the phone. If the intent for this choice is to force accountability through written communication, it might be a sign that something else is not right. Staff might be dodging responsibility for fear of punishment, internally competing with each other, or lacking commitment to the organization. That is not to say that indirect communication does not have its own value—especially written communication. In many instances, communication should be recorded and saved for later use.

Certainly, technology has greatly improved indirect interaction by introducing live video into the mix. However, it still cannot generate the level of completeness that in-person experience provides. There is just no way of replacing direct, face-to-face human contact, either one-on-one or in group settings.

Through the interpersonal work domain, managers address both formal and informal spheres of the organization. Indirect interactions tend to be more useful in the formal sphere, while direct ones tend to contribute more to the informal sphere.

In short, the quality of the interpersonal work in an organization has a major impact on everybody's performance. Managers should be conscious of which human qualities contribute to the enrichment of interpersonal interactions and push for an organizational culture that values cohesiveness, by appropriately using the management functions that are best suited to this work domain.

3.3   *Work Group Work Domain*

Work groups[2] do not have a fixed delimitation, but they are often defined as a group of people consisting of a manager and the manager's direct reports.

Although individuals in such groups maintain regular direct or indirect contact with each other, and their work is somewhat closely related, their deliverables are often treated as isolated responsibilities. In such a situation, an individual may go home after completing his assignments for the day, while a co-worker who uses the first worker's deliverables as input and runs into unrelated problems must stay longer to finish his own work. In this example, the first worker has no accountability in relation to the performance of the second worker. Ultimately, their managers administer rewards and penalties based mainly on dissociated appraisals of each direct report's performance.

By observing, analyzing, and understanding the features and dynamics of work groups, managers can empower themselves to better address and overcome obstacles. For example, how can team spirit be created when deliverables are treated independently? Some possible answers to this question could be:

- By involving their direct reports in planning and problem solving

- By distributing work in ways that increase the integration of the work group

- By defining issues that the work group can tackle together

- By implementing a reward system that takes into account the work group's collective deliverables

Another possible way to improve managers' handling of work groups is by contrasting it with teams. By doing so, managers may be able to see what adaptations[*] need to be made to the different management functions, tools, approach, and so forth.

3.4 Team Work Domain

Unlike in work groups, in teams[3], individual deliverables cannot be considered complete unless they are comingled with the deliverables of the other members. In other words, an adequate team deliverable cannot be obtained by the efforts of just some of its members. It has to be the result of a collective endeavor.

The generation of adequate deliverables by teams requires a special mindset that induces group cohesion and a spirit of collaboration far superior to what is usually found in work groups. It is precisely this finer attitude, this spirit of partnership, that managers try to elicit when encouraging teamwork in work group contexts.

The big challenge here is to transcend the simple "sum" of parts (individuals) and embrace the notion that a team is a unit. Part of the data that allows for this understanding of a team as a single entity comes from observing the dynamics and results of decisions made in groups. If correctly executed, such a decision-making process can be seen as the workings of a single collective mind that can produce more complete and superior results than those of a collage of individual thoughts.

Due to the difficulties in working at this high level of integration where separate individuals "morph" into a single unit, it is not uncommon for people to end up creating sub-units within the team. A representation that helps to visualize such sub-units and can assist in gauging team performance is the "I, WE, and IT" model. This model depicts team stages by taking into consideration the level of unity adopted by team members.

The "I" stage is the most immature stage. It is more like a pseudo team. At this stage, teams exist more due to external imposition rather than to intellectual and/or emotional affiliation of their members. Here, team

---

[*] Adaptations often need to be made to all management elements in every work domain.

members have a hard time agreeing on common goals, as personal agendas often take precedence. Teams at this stage are very dysfunctional and can hardly produce anything unless pressed by external forces.

Figure 3.4.a: The "I" Stage

At the "We" stage, team members agree on common goals to some extent, but do so without giving up their personal objectives. Members work towards common goals by trying to accommodate their individual needs among themselves and with the team's agenda. It is more like a negotiation stage than a collaborative one. Members feel some affiliation to the team, but their individuality is still so strong that they can easily clash with each other or reconsider their participation in the team. At this stage, teams constantly revisit decisions, and lots of energy is dissipated. The work of teams at this level proceeds with two steps forward and one step backward.

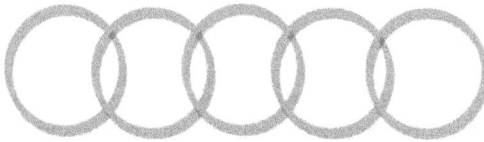

Figure 3.4.b: The "WE" Stage

The highest stage is the "IT" stage. At this stage, members place the team's goals entirely above their own. Individual ideas become the property of the group, making grievance-free testing of these ideas possible. Members develop a level of affinity that allows synergy to flourish. The team reaches the stage of a unit, of a single entity. It acquires a personality of its own.

Figure 3.4.c: The "IT" Stage

Of course, these three stages are just an outline of possibilities. In practice, on a given team there may be team members at different levels. For example, two members may be at the "IT" stage, four at the "WE" stage, and one at the "I" stage. Furthermore, members can move back and forth, especially between the "I" and "WE" stages. However, once a member reaches the capacity to perform at the "IT" stage, such a person rarely moves down to a lower stage again.

A fundamental factor for increasing team performance, then, is the capacity of the individual members to pass beyond the "I" and "WE" stages and operate at the "IT" stage. Among other things, this transition requires higher and higher levels of humility, detachment, and patience.

We should bear in mind that, like in the analogy of the human body, the concept of a team does not call for homogeneity. The governing principle is unity in diversity. Submission to the will of the group does not mean annihilation of the self.

Some practical examples of management elements that need to be adjusted for this domain are:

- Monitoring
- Supporting
- Rewards and Penalties

Like what often happens with work groups, a classical management mistake that tends to be counterproductive is the arrangement of an exclusively individual reward and penalty system applied to the team domain.

A change of paradigm is required to manage a team properly, and/or to participate fittingly as one of its members. Definitely, a paradigm that is materialistic and individualistic does not favor teamwork.

3.5 Task Work Domain

In the context of an organization, a task[4] is the most elementary piece of work. Tasks are the building blocks of the overall organizational venture. They should generate distinct deliverables, which should eventually be combined with other deliverables to create a more relevant and complete result. In isolation, a task has little value, since it rarely satisfies an ultimate need. For instance, the creation of a report can be seen as a task, which by itself does not have much value. Still, a report needs to be analyzed, and eventually action should probably be taken.

Tasks are carried out either by executing the transformation or the transfer phase of a process (see section 3.11). Sometimes, though, a long series of transformations and transfers is also labeled as task. For example, the physical delivery of mail around an office building can be seen as a task that corresponds to a single transfer phase of a process. However, the sorting plus the delivery of the same mail, which could be considered the "transformation", and the transfer phases, respectively, can be said to comprise the single task of mail delivery.

Thus, a task does not have a uniform boundary. Boundaries are determined by an organization's internal decisions, which can depend on factors like strategy, volume of the task, complexity of the task, and organizational provisions. In general, the fewer provisions an organization has, the less complexity it has and the larger the task boundaries can be.

Although everyone in an organization is responsible for tasks, when a task becomes overwhelming for one individual to handle, it can be split among a group of people. For instance, the task of calling a large number of clients can be split among several staff members or, using the example above, the task of sorting and delivering mail could be split between two or more people.

The task work domain can be very alluring, as it is easily discernible by the senses and generally presents a straightforward relationship with planning, execution, and outcome.

As a result, managers who tend to zoom through subjective work run the greatest risk of being entangled with tasks, eventually dedicating disproportionally more attention and energy to the task than to any other work domain. This excessive focus on individual tasks can cause a manager to constantly get directly involved with the execution of a task under a direct report's responsibility. This type of management ultimately interferes with the productivity of the direct report.

Managers should never forget that work assigned to direct reports becomes the direct reports' responsibility, not theirs, even though they are co-responsible for the outcome. In fact, it is right to expect that the direct reports should come to know how to perform their own work better than their managers. As one of Honda Corporation's principles goes, "The world's greatest experts are on-the-spot"[5]. If this is not the case in an organization, it may be a sign that something is wrong. Examples include direct reports who are not qualified, could need training, or might be receiving corrupted input, or managers who could be wrongly assigning work. If managers check on their direct reports' tasks every 5 minutes, fixing little details, then it is preferable and more efficient for the manager to do the work him or herself.

A manager's correct approach to his or her direct reports' work is not an issue of management style—that is, it is not an issue of a manager being autocratic, hands off, participative, or paternalistic. It is not even a matter of desire for control, a lack of trust in direct reports, or a drive for perfection. It is a matter of a manager correctly relating to the diverse work domains and correctly performing the different management functions, in order to make the execution of individual and collective work possible by their direct reports.

If a manager is capable of focusing on other work domains besides tasks, he or she feels compelled to distribute his or her attention between them all. Certainly, such a manager will not permit him or herself to be counting the pennies and forgetting to watch over the billions.

3.6 Activity Work Domain

An activity[6] is a group of closely related tasks that, together, should generate deliverables of aggregate value. It is one level up from a task, in terms of the complexity of work, and with the complexity comes less perception by the senses. In this domain, a higher level of intellectual exertion, supported by tools like tables, charts and maps, is required for managers to be able to adequately facilitate the operation. Like tasks, activities do not have standard boundaries and are subject to the same internal organizational decision criteria.

Activities are primarily formed when managers try to address the first stage of significant increase in diversity and complexity of work. The objective is the creation of work areas that are more specialized and, therefore, more efficient and manageable. For example, a small organization might have a single individual handling a group of somewhat related tasks to take care of its finances, such as receiving payments, paying bills and depositing money in the bank. As the organization grows, each task becomes more and more complex. Receiving payments, for example, at some point will not be done exclusively on a cash basis. It will also require tasks such as issuing collection statements, handling overdue payments, and monitoring clients' credit limits. In this case, these tasks warrant the creation of an activity conventionally referred to as Accounts Receivable. Furthermore, the other tasks will also be departmentalized into the areas of Accounts Payable and Current Assets Management, and each will be staffed with different people.

There are also times when a single task can be targeted for departmentalization due to the volume of work. For example, the task of trying to collect overdue payments could be split off from the Accounts Receivable activity, or the task of making payments could be split between multiple people, forming a new work area. This makes the new area, although still a single task, similar to an activity, in terms of management needs.

With multiple direct reports assigned to a single activity, the execution of all management functions becomes more complex. In particular, managers are required to pay more attention to the connections between the diverse workstations and the workstations with external work areas and agents. Consequently, they must increase the use of the functions of Coordinating and Cultural Modeling.

When a single person or team handles an activity, regardless of whether the direct report is a non-manager, a manager, or a managing team, managers should treat the activity the same way they treat tasks handled by single individuals. Like with tasks, managers should make sure that activities assigned to direct reports are their duty, playing a peripheral role and not getting involved with the execution of activities[*]. For instance, managers should facilitate the flow of input and output between the activity and external work areas, but not the flow of input and output between the tasks inside the activity.

The main factor regulating the application of management functions in this work domain is the number of direct reports, and not the number of existing workstations and tasks in the domain.

---

[*] This should not be confused with situations in small organizations where managers often perform both managerial and non-managerial work.

3.7 Functional Area Work Domain

A functional area[7] is formed when a manager clusters correlated activities in the process of departmentalization. Consequently, a functional area also has no standardized boundaries.

Functional areas, commonly referred to as departments, are universally labeled in accordance with their work specialization, such as Human Affairs (Resources), Finance, Marketing, and IT. Other factors like hierarchical status can lead to the assignment of areas as departments, even though these areas might not be the result of aggregated activities.

An example of a functional area could be a Marketing Department that is composed of the following activities: Brand Management, Market Research, Promotion (publicity and advertising), Sales, and Client/Customer Relations.

As expected, the level of subjectivism that managers have to deal with in functional areas is even higher than it is for activities. Boundaries are broader; there are more deliverables and internal and external connections. The work becomes especially challenging in the informal sphere, as the increase in the number of direct and indirect reports increases human dynamics. In summary, aggregated work becomes more complex.

A manager's primary duty in a functional area is the performance of management functions in relation to the activities. That being the case, managers should be even more dissociated from tasks, especially as they begin to have other managers as direct reports.

With so much work under a single manager, odds are that the demands for management functions are high enough to consume most, if not all, of a manager's time and energy. In other words, managers should devote less time to performing non-managerial work themselves. Consequently, a more enhanced execution of management functions becomes even more necessary, and can be achieved through measures like deeper management acumen, greater reliance on theoretical models, and management tools.

As discussed before, there is no limit to the number of areas and levels that can be created. This means that the process of grouping and forming more and more complex structures can potentially go on indefinitely. Beyond functional areas, the departmentalization process tends to move towards the creation of branches arranged in a matrix structure, and after that, to the creation of business units.

The capacity to understand and observe the incremental changes in the work of ever-enlarging domains is at the basis of a manager's performance. Such a requirement is especially relevant when a manager has to accommodate his or her work to a particular management level and specific processes.

3.8 Geographical Work Domain

The geographical[8] domain refers to the physical location where the formal sphere of work is executed. Work can be carried out at a single site or dispersed locally, regionally, globally, or even into outer space.

What is relevant here is dispersed work, which is usually the result of organizational growth. Because relatively few organizations grow to a size that becomes strategically interesting enough to disperse, many managers never get to experience this facet of the geographical work domain. One of the consequences is that there is relatively little public knowledge available that managers can draw upon to help them improve their performance in such a setting.

In addition to this lack of public knowledge, there is a tendency to dedicate more attention to things that stimulate our senses. As the saying goes, "out of sight, out of mind". It is somewhat common for many managers to have difficulty adjusting the execution of their management functions when faced with a transition from concentrated to dispersed work.

A common and rather natural inclination seems to be for managers handling dispersed work to try to find ways to imitate the management of a single site. Among other things, this effort, guided by a well-designed and rigorously implemented schedule, implies frequent interactions assisted by technology and regular visits to external sites. When this approach is not systematically implemented, or it generates little result, decentralization tends to be the default outcome with the diverse locations linked to each other mainly by way of top hierarchical levels.

Unwanted consequences resulting from inadequate management of external physical locations might not be as related to the formal sphere as it could be to the informal. Usually it is relatively easier to deal with formal components from a distance than it is to handle informal ones, especially if there is a lack of maturity when interacting with cultural diversity inside the organization. Imagine, for example, the case of an organization that has branches in different geographical locations populated by different ethnic groups. Management across such cultural boundaries requires a level of maturity that cannot be dependent on science alone.

A possible good path for the integration of dispersed geographic locations is through interactions between managers, followed by an increase in direct interactions between non-managers. In other words, the relationship and scheme of work between managers needs to be developed first; otherwise, no stable geographic integration can be achieved. Once accomplished, it should be followed by the establishment of channels that allow for direct interactions between direct reports with as little interference from their managers as possible. For example, if a report prepared by a non-manager is to be used by another non-manager in another location, a direct connection should be established between these two.

By allowing and encouraging the development of relationships at all levels between all locations, the increase in general understanding and camaraderie greatly facilitates geographic integration. These efforts, backed up by fair treatment of all locations, have as their final goal the creation and maintenance of a single organizational identity that complements the local ones.

Supporting and Cultural Modeling are the functions quite possibly most affected by the differences in geographical work arrangements. Thus, managers should be conscious of which adjustments they need to make to these and the other functions in order to continue effectively carrying out their duties.

3.9 Virtual Work Domain

The cyber-technology environment characterizes the virtual work[9] domain. This domain can be used by people working in a single physical location or dispersed throughout multiple sites. Like the geographical domain, it too becomes trickier from a management perspective when direct reports are dispersed.

Because it can eliminate reliance on an organization's physical facilities, it permits even greater scattering than the geographical domain, often causing individual workers to become isolated.

This domain is especially suited for non-managerial work. This means that managers involved with intensive virtual work often deal with direct reports who are carrying out tasks and activities, and not with other managers.

Again, the organization's formal sphere is less of an issue here. Tools that assist with Planning, Coordinating, and Monitoring, such as web-based project planning, workflow, and issue tracking tools, abound in the field of cyber-technology. Certainly, these tools do not replace managers, but they can greatly enhance their performance.

Supplementary steps, like a clear definition of the rules of interaction, an upfront meticulous analysis of expected deliverables, and a rational utilization of specific communication mediums, are also measures that can contribute to the management of this domain.

As seen before in the geographical domain, the hardest thing for managers to do in a setting where their direct reports are dispersed is for them to adjust their functions to deal satisfactorily with the organization's informal sphere. If in more traditional contexts managers already tend to pay less attention to the informal sphere than they do to the formal, then in a situation where in-person interaction is almost non-existent it is quite understandable that managers will have an even harder time focusing on the informal issues.

Certainly, it can be hard to create good rapport with direct reports in a virtual work domain, but managers need to make an extra effort to address this matter. Perhaps, above all, managers should control themselves so as not to become unsympathetic and/or unfriendly in their relationship with their direct reports. At the very least, managers can occasionally take time to connect and chat with their direct reports about subjects unrelated to business. Again, whenever possible, personal contact is very much advised.

Even if managers happen to be satisfied with the material results obtained from what might seem to be almost exclusively formal interactions, if the informal sphere is not deliberately addressed, it can be very difficult to have direct reports really committed to the organization. Typically, in such a situation, a direct report's commitment will only be as strong as his or her financial interest.

Notwithstanding a distant virtual association, direct reports are part of the organization, and to some extent, they too help shape its culture, thus affecting its mission.

3.10 Outsourcing Work Domain

Unlike buying products from suppliers or hiring contractors to fill sporadic needs for consulting or technical repair, outsourcing[10] is the commissioning of a third party or parties, for a part of a business' regular operation that is strategically categorized as secondary, or not directly linked to the core business.

Unfortunately, as much as some managers would like to divest themselves completely of the responsibilities over some work areas by outsourcing, in practice this cannot be 100% satisfactorily achieved.

There are diverse setups for such an operational arrangement, but broadly speaking, managers can approach outsourcing as either in-house or external. The differences between these two setups can greatly affect what outsourcing managers are able to do.

Setting aside the management function of (strategic) Planning, with its rationalizations for outsourcing, two issues relevant to the execution of several other management functions are as follows:

a. Outsourced personnel could end up having more than one manager (matrix), in the event that outsourcing managers get involved with the outsourced operational processes.

b. Outsourcing managers might interact directly with some outsourced personnel but have very constrained or no managerial responsibilities over them. This might include partial control over turnover—that is, outsourcing managers may request that personnel be replaced, but have no say over hiring. Another common challenge for outsourcing managers is ensuring that outsourced personnel are adequately available. This can easily happen when all outsourced personnel are housed externally and they do not work exclusively for one organization. The economic ranking of their clients is one issue that can influence their availability.

Along these lines,

- It is important that both the outsourcing and outsourced managers develop good working relations and constantly review and improve their management boundaries.

- The outsourcing and outsourced organizations should align their strategies as much as possible. In fact, the outsourcing organization should try to acculturate the outsourced personnel as much as possible, especially if they are stationed in-house. This idea of acculturation might sound odd to some, but if, for instance, the two organizations give different priorities to the formal and informal spheres, or to values and operation, or to deliverables (what) and process (how), differences such as these in organizational cultures could eventually create problems.

Finally, when taken to the extreme level of management disengagement, outsourcing can result in a setup that is equivalent to that of suppliers or contractors being locked into long-term agreements. In such scenarios, the outsourcing organization can end up mistakenly believing that it is possible to focus only on the outsourced companies' final deliverables rather than on joint management.

3.11   Process Work Domain

A process[11] is a sustained phenomenon marked by a series of changes that succeed one another in a relatively fixed way and lead toward a particular end or result.

In an organization, then, a process can be seen as a "whole", made up of a concatenation of at least two distinctive phases that alternate with each other: transformation and transfer.

For any phase of a process to come into being, one or more tasks must be executed—that is, tasks are equally applicable to both transformation and transfer. Indeed, tasks can be micro systems in their own right, with their own processes. According to this concept, there is no such thing as separate tasks and processes, and managers do not have the "luxury" to consider themselves only a task or a process person.

From a manager's perspective, results are only achieved after goods or services are progressively developed through a series of steps that cut across different work areas. In a macro example, an airline company prepares airplanes, sells tickets, boards the passengers, transports them, de-planes them, and unloads the passengers' belongings at their final destinations. While all these areas are systems on their own with their own processes and deliverables, to top managers, the service is only complete when they manage to integrate all the above areas successfully.

In management, a common approach for dealing with processes has been to divide them into three parts: input, transformation, and output.

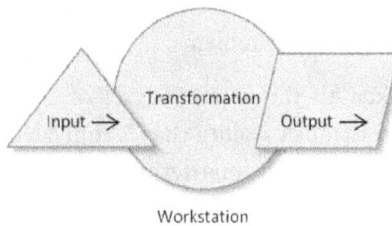

Figure 3.11.a: Focus on Workstation

Unfortunately, if a manager looks at these three parts primarily as dimensions of an individual work area or workstation, this approach can easily reinforce the manager's attention on a direct report's tasks. In other words, it is easy to focus on the input that workstation X receives, then on the transformation that it causes on the input received, and finalize the "process" with focus on the output delivered by the workstation. In this case, workstation X dominates most of the manager's attention. What is being relegated to a position of less importance is the transfer, or transition from one work area to another.

To avoid this excessive focus on single workstations and better deal with processes, managers should keep in mind that they must address two distinctive types of phases. This should help managers broaden their vision to adopt a methodical approach to the transfer phase.

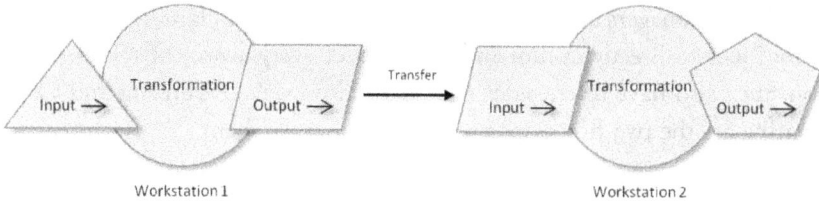

Figure 3.11.b: Focus on Transfer

An intermediary workstation might exist with the sole purpose of assisting with transfer—that is, it might operate without performing any relevant transformation.

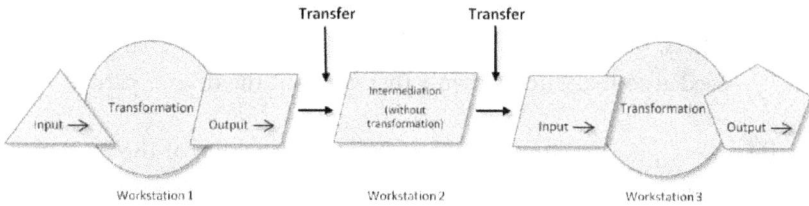

Figure 3.11.c: Focus on Transfers

Broadly speaking, from a management perspective, it does not matter if a workstation is going to transform or just serve as an intermediary. Organizing has equal concern for every workstation, and Coordinating connects them all without partiality.

Consequently, processes should primarily be dealt with, on one hand, by executing the function of Organizing to address transformation (and intermediation), and on the other hand, by executing the function of Coordinating to attend to transfer.

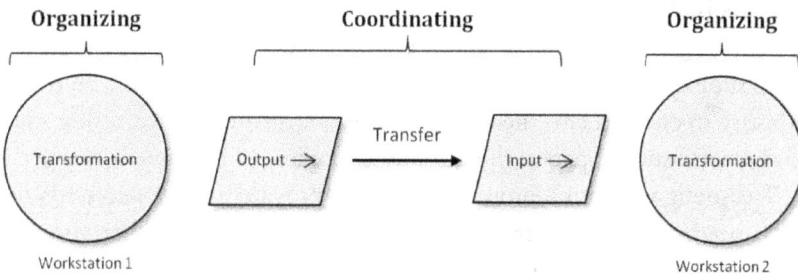

Figure 3.11.d: Phases of a Process Handled by Organizing and Coordinating

When managers are executing other functions like Planning and Monitoring, which directly and/or indirectly affect every aspect of the organization, they also have to consider processes. However, Organizing and Coordinating are the two functions specialized to handle them.

Contrary to common practice, of the two phases, the transfer phase is the one that should require the more frequent intervention from the manager. The reason for this is twofold:

1. A transfer is prone to more fluctuation

2. As a transition phase, it addresses the concerns of two or more parties, where in many instances no individual has authority over the others. Consequently, it is often the case that external authority is needed to make adjustments that best suit the diverse parties.

Because a process often entails many steps, it is one of the hardest domains for managers to visualize. Fortunately, especially for those who have difficulty in dealing with processes, nobody should be disheartened by this difficulty, because there are tools that help in the visualization of processes.

The most common tool used for mapping processes is a flowchart[12]. There are different models of flowcharts, but they are all graphic illustrations that use standardized symbols to depict the flow of work. These charts portray the workflow in tasks, activities, functional areas, and so forth. Although flowcharts provide a good view of the breakdown of transformation, they can become even more helpful if managers add some detail to them about the transfer phases.

To deal specifically with transfers, forms[13] are at the top of the list as useful tools. The creation of new forms or the examination of existing ones can also assist in the analysis and design, or redesign, of processes. Several things should be considered when working with forms, such as who has the authority to create them, their standardization, instructions for using them, the characteristics of paper, the number of copies, and if digital, interactivity. Well-designed forms prompt people to provide all the necessary data that is needed at the next transformation stage of a process. They also eliminate the waste of energy and, above all, reduce conflicts.

A special note must be made regarding deliverables in the form of information, ideas, or feelings that are communicated directly from individuals to individuals. In these cases, since humans themselves serve as mediums, and deliverables flow in the form of words and body language, it is not only helpful but also paramount that managers, back by their authority, wisely and justly watch over such transferences. The manner in which people in organizations carry themselves and communicate with others becomes a relevant characteristic of a medium for transferring deliverables.

Processes that incorporate more than one work area are the responsibility of managers, even though in some organizations their actual mapping may be delegated to direct reports or to a department that specializes in this job. In the end, the importance for every manager to be able to properly visualize, understand, and work with processes cannot be overemphasized.

3.12 Management Level Work Domain

A management level[14] is a boundary formed by adaptations made to management functions. It should be noted that the list of functions is the same for every management level. However, at different levels, functions tend to vary in both characteristics and apportioning. Furthermore, these variations are not standardized throughout all organizations. Final variations and the number of levels depend on many factors such as organization size, complexity of production, strategy, political decisions, and management acumen.

For instance, at the lowest management level, the function of Monitoring a production line should be carried out around the clock, while at the top level, the Monitoring of the organization's performance might only be weekly, monthly, or quarterly. Not only does the apportioning of time vary among management levels, but the attributes, tools, and managers' approach used to execute such duties differ as well.

Although the number of management levels is conventionally set at around three to four, larger organizations can have additional hierarchical layers, or sub-levels, at each management level. Furthermore, each level can also have anywhere from a few to many managers. In contrast, small organizations could possibly have only one level of management, with or without direct reports. In the case of a one-person business, a single individual has to perform managerial functions, like Planning and Provisioning, and execute non-managerial work. Thus, business owners without direct reports have to produce deliverables from diverse areas, such as operations, finance, and marketing.

In any case, as organizations grow, the distribution of staff surrenders to the pyramid principle. Consequently, higher levels have fewer managers and direct reports, whereas lower levels have more managers and direct reports.

The most common practice is to abstractly divide management into three levels: top-level, middle-level, and lower-level.

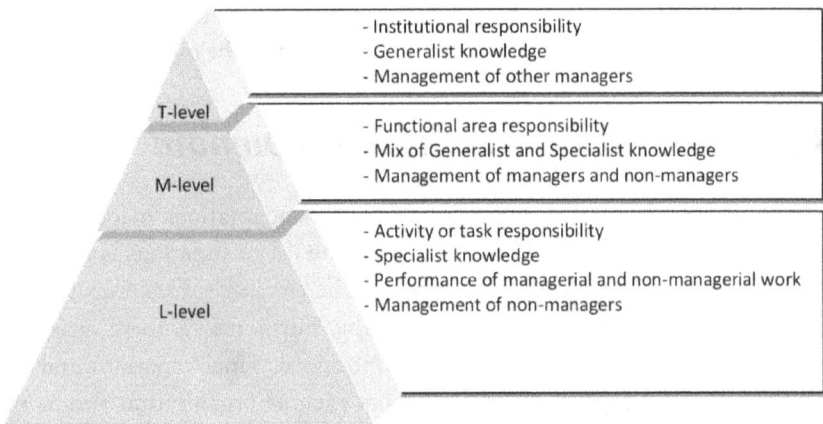

T-level
- Institutional responsibility
- Generalist knowledge
- Management of other managers

M-level
- Functional area responsibility
- Mix of Generalist and Specialist knowledge
- Management of managers and non-managers

L-level
- Activity or task responsibility
- Specialist knowledge
- Performance of managerial and non-managerial work
- Management of non-managers

Figure 3.12: Management Levels

- Top-level managers seldom manage non-managers, with the common exception of assistants and advisors, and almost never perform non-managerial work. In general, they deal with large work areas, such as an entire organization or business unit.

- Middle-level managers manage other managers, or a combination of managers and non-managers, and might perform some non-managerial work. In general, they deal with functional areas.

- Lower-level managers mainly manage non-managers and tend to perform non-managerial work themselves. In general, they deal with non-managers handling activities or tasks.

The differences in types and numbers of direct reports, plus the range of areas under each manager's responsibility, are the main reasons for variations in management functions. For example, at the lower levels, managers tend to deal with a greater number of staff performing somewhat similar jobs. Such a context requires, for instance, more attention to coordination. On the other hand, at higher levels, managers interact with fewer staff performing much more diversified duties, which necessitates more planning.

Often managers adhere to the dynamics of each level without much thinking, mainly driven by impositions created by departmentalization. This should not lead one to assume that a solid understanding of the concept of management levels happens naturally. A manager's ability to visualize and adapt to management levels is a must-have skill that needs to be developed. In the absence of this skill, there will be frequent deviations from the characteristics of management functions demanded by each level.

One common deviation is that of managers of higher levels performing as if they were lower-level managers, such as board directors dedicating more time to issues of coordination and organization than to planning.

The construct of management levels is also commonly used to determine pay, with titles adopted for each level varying from industry to industry and from country to country. As globalization progresses, these differences are slowly disappearing, with titles becoming more related to the best practices in management. That said, the main purpose of the concept of management levels should be to assist managers to perform satisfactorily, and in line with the requirements imposed by their position in the organizational structure.

PART II

Managing

4

Management Functions

Management is a function of the division of labor[1]. In other words, with the advent of and subsequent increase in the complexity of the division of labor, a special occupation became necessary to assist the divided work to function as a unit.

Over time, like everything else in this contingent world, management has also evolved. It has evolved because of factors like the size and complexity of enterprises, technology levels, levels of stress placed on managers, societal contexts, and human maturity. In spite of evolution, the essence of management remains the same. Even change in management level, functional area and industry do not alter the essence of management. The characteristics of management functions[2] can vary, and they should be employed to a greater of lesser degree according to where a manager is positioned. Still, management is a single reality.

Thus, a definition of management that acknowledges its essence and reconciles it with the concept of human beings as social and spiritual beings could be:

*Management is the endeavor of facilitating the collective pro-
duction of deliverables*

Such an endeavor is characterized by a set of specific functions performed by individuals or teams who occupy hierarchical positions with ad-
vantageous viewpoints in the structure of an organization. This arrangement
allows individuals or team managers to assume macro duties over the fields
covered by their "visions". These fields can contain either parts of or the
entirety of social enterprises, and they can even relate to some areas external
to the organization. Ultimately, the aim is for management to facilitate the
integration and resulting dynamics between the jobs that have been divided,
in order to produce collective deliverables.

Notwithstanding the usual attention focused on ongoing production,
this facilitation effort spans the entire organizational life cycle, including the
formation and dissolution phases. On a daily basis however, managers
should center their focus on the maintenance and advancement of the organization.

One of the implications of this management concept is that managers
are co-accountable for the result of people's work affected by their facilitation effort. This co-accountability exists regardless of whether management
functions are carried out with or without the involvement of direct reports.
Managers cannot avoid the fact that whatever they do affects—not only
positively but also negatively—the work of their direct reports and the organization as a whole.

A modest but nonetheless fitting example in assisting with the visualization of this unique role played by management is that of a manager who is
little, or not at all, involved with the execution of the work assigned to his
or her direct reports. By not being directly involved with the execution of
the work performed at a particular workstation, the manager has the perspective, time and opportunity to see what is going on at other workstations. In doing so, the manager is in a better position to try to figure out
how to fix and improve things from a macro perspective.

Suppose, for instance, that workstation E is not performing well, due to
inconsistencies in the quality of the input that it is receiving. By diagnosing
and analyzing the issue, management concludes that the source of the prob-

lem is located at workstation B (several workstations before E). In such a context, it would probably prove very disruptive if the staff of workstation E were to try to solve the problem on its own. On the other hand, workstation E could be empowered to address certain issues directly with workstations immediately adjacent to it, such as workstations D and F.

It is important to keep in mind that even though managers have the best view, they cannot see everything, especially in very complex and dynamic systems. Consequently, the concept of direct report involvement with the execution of management is not only desirable, but also important. This idea of direct report involvement can be further corroborated by the principle of justice and the fact that, although it is not practical for everybody to be responsible for every single phase of the production process, everybody is, nonetheless, collectively responsible for the well-being of the organization.

Management functions can be divided into three groups: leadership function, core functions, and complementary functions.

1. Leadership Function

    Initiates the process of the unification of people around a single undertaking and maintains the unity of the group.

2. Core Functions

    a. *Planning* – Plans work, regardless of the range.

    b. *Organizing* – Further details the organization of work and the specifications of necessary provisions.

    c. *Provisioning* – Acquires externally, and/or develops in-house, the necessary provisions to execute the work, and positions them in accordance with what has been planned and organized.

    d. *Coordinating* – Coordinates the flow of deliverables between workstations and between the organization and external agents.

3. Complementary Functions

    a. *Monitoring* – Monitors the state of the provisions and functioning of the system against a societal backdrop, making adjustments as needed.

b. *Supporting* – Supports direct reports and others when feasible, including external agents, to ensure well-being, improve performance, and enable the organization to progress.

c. *Cultural Modeling* – Models the culture to ensure that direct reports in the work area, and consequently in the organization, have the right posture for sustaining a performance that is in line with the strategy.

d. *Liaising* – Acts as a liaison between own area(s) of responsibility and other internal and external areas.

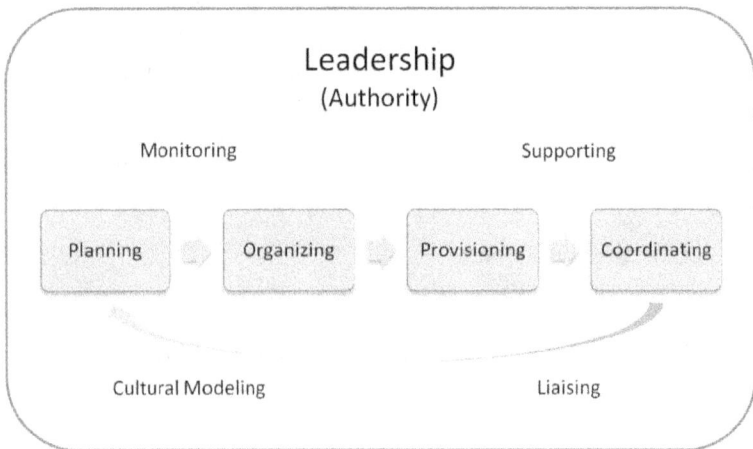

Figure 4: Management Functions

In practice, it is not easy to visualize this departmentalized and sequential exposition of management functions, especially given the following:

*   *The reality of management levels* – This reality creates several parallel management cycles in an organization, each often being affected by, and sometimes a bit off-pace in relation to, the others. For example, operational planning can only be initiated by lower level management after top level management has concluded the strategic planning and has moved on to perform other functions. As such, it is also possible that the lower level management has most, if not all, of its provisions already defined by upper management, which implies that lower level Provisioning has been carried out before Planning.

- *The conceptual stage of functions* – The conceptual stage of some functions should be addressed before their implementation. For instance, the conceptual work of Organizing should come before Provisioning. Provisioning before conceptual Organizing indicates the lack of a plan. In this regard, during Planning, a reasonable amount of conceptualization should be accomplished for Organizing, Provisioning, Coordinating, and so forth.

- *The scattered execution of management functions for the purpose of maintenance* – The scattered execution of management functions also occurs throughout all management levels during ongoing operations, ideally for the purpose of maintenance. These actions, generally resulting from Monitoring, are often carried out in meetings with the intention of adjusting the other diverse management deliverables. For example, the need to adjust cash flow can require a targeted execution of Planning and Provisioning.

- *The difference between ongoing operation and projects, regardless of size* – During ongoing operations, all management functions at all management levels are cyclical. Furthermore, all management functions should occasionally be tapped as part of the continuing maintenance and development of the system, even though their phase in a cycle has already passed. This is not always the case with projects, which are generally expected to be non-cyclical.

4.1 Leadership Function

Leadership[3] is as much a topic of exceptional interest in the management world as it is a challenging one.

To start, the word leadership represents different things. Sometimes it signifies a hierarchical position, other times a capacity or ability. It is also synonymous with authority, and even with management.

For our purpose, the key discussion is the one that revolves around the question of how leadership relates to management. A large group sees leadership as a management function, while others see it as a possible evolution of management.

For those who see leadership as a possible evolution of management, the expectation is the replacement of managers with leaders. Unfortunately, it seems unrealistic to expect that leaders, as described by this group, should focus on some aspects of management and ignore others. This is especially true at lower management levels. Imagine, for instance, new staff, with little knowledge and experience, being motivated to accomplish visions and objectives without someone assisting with Organizing, Coordinating, and Monitoring. In other words, the duties that are associated with leadership do not cover all management needs.

Perhaps much of the desired evolution that many would like to see taking place stems from expectations for a change of attitude by managers. This change would then be reflected by how managers exercise their authority, or how they carry out their duties: with fairness, respect, direct report involvement, and so on.

Though managers might be controlling, rude, or dictatorial, their transformation into leaders will not solve the main underlying problem. The driving force behind satisfying one's ego by being number one, gaining power, privileges, and the capacity to boss people around can be found in both the "lust for leadership"[4] and in dictatorial management. It is not without reason that, throughout history, the lust for leadership has been one of the greatest sources of problems for humanity. Although this problem has historically been recorded in connection with the affairs of religion and government, it tends to occur in organizational settings as well.

This means that at its heart, leadership, even in an organizational setting, is not immune from precisely the same dysfunctional human behavior sometimes observed in dictatorial management. Contrary to the reality of an organization, a selfish individual will always try to satisfy his or her own personal interests over those of the group, no matter what it takes. The means might change, but the final objective is still the same: exclusive personal gratification. Such a person will definitely not hesitate to exploit others. This predicament begets the question of which alternative is better: to be controlled by a dictatorial manager or to be manipulated by a charismatic leader?

Fortunately, it is also possible to find leaders and managers who position themselves as instruments of collective well-being. Clearly, the problem is not with leadership or management per se, but how humans choose to carry out these services.

The relevance of leadership should not be overlooked just because it might be misused. On the contrary, leadership is necessary to initiate and facilitate unifying processes and to help align actions in collective endeavors. For example, if five people simultaneously try to start a meeting with different topics, locations, and so forth, steps to adjust all these events will be extremely complicated. It is also often the case that when responsibility is distributed among too many people, nothing happens. On the other hand, if one person initiates the process, it is much easier for all to accept a single invitation, adjust individual schedules and thus help create an initial unifying movement.

It may be correct to consider leadership the first management function, the function that initiates things, that takes the first step. This does not mean that there should not be space for individual direct report initiative. Individual initiative of direct reports should be encouraged within their spheres of responsibility.

Because social advancement is moving towards collective involvement, other duties attributed to leadership, such as presenting visions, establishing objectives, and providing plans, are becoming less and less the responsibility of single individuals and are turning more and more into collective endeavors.

In fact, it is impossible for anyone, including a top manager, to claim that an idea was his or hers alone. For instance, if a person claims to have had the idea of building the first skyscraper, it is because someone has already had the idea of building a high-rise, and before that a lower-rise, a house, a tent, and moving into a cave, perhaps by following the example of animals. In the end, "success (always) has many fathers".

The point is that on this physical plane, human development requires social interaction. Left alone and uneducated, if humans manage to survive like wild animals, they cannot progress and produce anything. For that reason, we must be just and humble, and accept that individual contributions are dependent on our interactions with our surroundings.

> *Man is organic with the world. His inner life moulds the environment and is itself also deeply affected by it. The one acts upon the*

*other and every abiding change in the life of man is the result of these
mutual reactions.*[5]

From a letter written on behalf of Shoghi Effendi

Consequently, it would be ideal for undertakings like creating a vision
or deciding what direction to take to be carried out collectively through a
management function like planning. Of course, such undertakings need to
accommodate practicality. In the context of extremely large groups, universal participation is more easily achieved through indirect channels, while in
small groups it can be realized through direct general participation. In any
case, it is always true that the more involvement there is in formulation, the
more commitment there is in execution.

That said, it is important and helpful to observe that the exercise of
leadership can adapt somewhat, depending on factors such as:

a) *The level of freedom individuals have in joining in collective endeavors*
   – In businesses, social contract requires a high level of acquiescence
   to leadership. This means that leadership in such a context does not
   need to rely as much on motivation, encouragement, empowerment, and so forth, in order to win participation. Nevertheless, and
   because management has other obligations, it is possible and perhaps beneficial to have those efforts be part of another function,
   such as Supporting.

b) *If leadership is carried out by an individual or by a group of people,
   such as in teams, committees, or assemblies* – Because institutions
   rarely have their members implementing decisions as a group, this
   peculiarity slightly decreases the need for individual members to
   publicly demonstrate a number of qualities related to the function
   of leadership. In fact, institution members should keep a lower profile and let the institution take center stage.

   On the other hand, because a low profile option is not so realistic in the case of leadership executed by single individuals, it is
   paramount for individuals exercising leadership to be good role
   models. More than anyone else, an individual leader must be able
   to exemplify what needs to be done. 'Do what I say, not what I do'
   is definitely not a principle conducive to collective action. The
   power of example is highly valued by all, especially in a context of
   collective effort where people are expected to share benefits and

deal with problems together. Managers must back up words with actions, or "walk the talk".

Aside from qualities like determination and perseverance, a leader must have the quality of courage as one of its distinguishing features. It is not unusual for managers to be afraid of taking action under difficult circumstances. On such occasions, they may try to ignore the problem, assign the issue to their direct reports, or deflect the matter to peers or superiors. If managers are truly to execute the function of leadership, it is essential that they have the courage to take the first step, even if it is just to gather everybody together for collective decision-making.

As a result, being a leader requires certain built-in qualities, though it is interesting to note that charm and special skills are not among them. One might or might not be extroverted, be a good speaker, like being the center of attention, and so forth. As long as a person's behavior is worthy of being emulated, then he or she can lead.

Let deeds, not words, be your adorning.[6]

Bahá'u'lláh

4.1.1 Authority

One of the requisites for the existence of order in an organization is differentiation among its members. Not all participants in an organization can be equal in degree.

Degrees are absolutely necessary to ensure an orderly organization.[7]

'Abdu'l-Bahá

One way that such differentiation in degree is obtained is through the power of authority. Without it, social enterprises eventually plunge into chaos and disintegrate. This being the case, any structure complying with the principle of "degrees" inevitably has to take on a hierarchical arrangement. Conversely, a flat organization, or any other structure that disregards this principle, is as unrealistic as anarchy.

As such, authority[8] is an integral ingredient of management. Lacking it, management functions might not be implementable. It is not feasible to lead, to play the role of facilitator, or to get involved in people's work without formal authority.

Regrettably, authority is often one of the trickiest and most difficult powers to be correctly executed, not to mention when it is used unlawfully.

In relation to society, the use of authority by organizational managers is relatively simple and straightforward, and is not a common source of challenge. For the most part, society does not care how authority shapes managers' performances inside organizations, or how they carry out their duties of Planning, Organizing, and so on. Society, through government, invests one or more people (in general top-level managers) with authority, primarily to officially represent the organization in dealings with external agents, such as suppliers, partners, customers, and government agencies.

Internally, however, authority becomes a problem when managers proceed with interventions without performing one or more of the core and/or complementary functions. Some examples of this are establishing directions for the organization without planning, prioritizing direct reports' tasks without taking into consideration the Organizing function—that is, without a clear vision of the direct reports' workload—and replacing direct reports based on personal reasons not at all related to the organization. In other words, the power of authority must not be employed as an end in itself. The purpose of authority is to serve as a means for making management functions workable. It empowers managers to implement plans, structures, connections, and so forth, which could easily become pointless if allowed to be opposed and modified by anyone at any given time.

Given this, it is easy to understand why this matter turns out to be a common cause of problems. Still, it is one thing to default to authority and use it as if it were a function, due to lack of knowledge. It is another thing to consciously misuse this power for personal advantage. The point is that authority must not be employed in isolation. When exercised, it must always be done in support of one or more management functions.

4.1.2 Authority vs. Decision Making

The power of authority stems from the prerogative of making decisions that become binding to others. Consequently, much of what is at the root of the improper use of management and leadership is the capacity to make decisions that disregard the concerns of others.

The search for ways to address this common problem is not new, and the attempt to segregate government functions into legislative, executive, and judiciary branches is a good example. In this case, the effort is to try to split the decision from the execution, and both from the arbitration. However, an even better step towards a more concrete solution can be found in the adoption and perfection of collective decision-making.

While a healthy exercise of authority by single individuals is heavily dependent on one's spiritual maturity, a marked decrease in the negative impact of selfish impulses can be achieved by constraining a person from making decisions alone.

In order to curtail the misuse of authority, adjustments in the organizational decision-making process must be made and complemented by a number of other concrete steps, like better policies and job descriptions and improvements in the process of filling in management positions.

This does not mean that management should be stripped of its authority or decision-making power. It means that management should embrace group decision-making as often as it is feasible.

One should not presume that for management functions to be carried out effectively, decision-making has to be concentrated on a single individual. In fact, as discussed before, the opposite is true. The more general involvement there is, the more successful management will be.

4.1.3 Problem Solving

There are many reasons why managers should have authority. Of these, the responsibility for addressing problems is one that deserves special attention.

> ...for each day there is a new problem and for every problem an expedient solution...[9]
>
> Bahá'u'lláh

As stated before, there are instances, especially in the macro context, when direct reports are ill-equipped to deal with certain difficulties. In such circumstances, managers are required to take action. This understanding should not be broadened to mean that managers should step in as omniscient saviors at any sign of trouble. In fact, when a problem is not the result of a person's flaw of character, and if it is first recognized in the sphere of responsibility of a particular direct report, the best approach is to coach and empower the individual to solve his or her own issues. That said, collective decision-making demands that empowered direct reports should also regularly seek managers' and co-workers' assistance.

When managers have to be the primary person responsible for problem solving, some of the common reasons are:

- *The problem is broad in scope* – The problem cannot be solved without addressing more workstations and areas than direct reports can handle.

- *The formal or informal, tangible or intangible cost of a problem is high, even though not immediately broad in scope* – Examples include the malfunctioning of key equipment or serious customer dissatisfaction. These problems might be resolved at the site without major repercussions, but they have the potential of reaching broader implications as well.

- *The timeframe for finding a solution is a critical factor* – The direct report does not have the luxury of time to find a solution to a problem. For example, there are occasional instances when timing does not allow for much margin of error, and elaborate consultation is not possible. This does not mean that consultation cannot take place at all. On such occasions, the highest authority should take charge, like in an airplane emergency. On the other hand, whenever possible, managers should not allow pressure to force hurried decisions.

- *The problem results from human conflict* – Even though some managers do not like to address human conflict, no manager can avoid addressing this type of problem. Managers have the obligation to take the first steps in solving human conflict to prevent its escalation and increased animosity between associates, and to return the work environment to a peaceful and productive setting as quickly as possible. In this regard, it must be emphasized that justice is one of the main means for solving human conflict.

Two simple ways for tackling problems are:

a. *Reversal of the problem statement* – Solutions can sometimes be found in the antithesis of the problem statement. Of course, this technique is pointless if the statement is false. For example, to reverse a statement is useless in a situation where what is being described is only a symptom of the problem.

b. *The "5-whys" Japanese technique* – It is an easy way to search for a cause of a problem. It works by posing the question of "why" to a problem. The obtained answer is again questioned with a "why" and the process is repeated several times until the sources of a problem are identified. This technique can help one look beyond symptoms.

One thing managers never have the right to do, even when a problem is encountered, is to treat direct reports with disrespect. There are no exceptions to this principle, even in circumstances where "mistakes" can greatly affect the organization. To mistreat others is utterly unacceptable. Not only is disrespect improper in dealings among human beings, but as managers disrespectfully try to disentangle themselves from problems to which they are intrinsically connected, they show signs of despotism and arrogance. Managers are not free from errors. Nor do they like to be mistreated when they make mistakes. If managers regularly misuse their authority in despotic ways, direct reports usually end up lying, hiding problems, deflecting responsibility, sabotaging work, and/or leaving the organization.

The truth is, since managers are part of operations, there is no way they can completely exclude themselves from some degree of accountability when it comes to mistakes made by direct reports. Even in the eventuality of reoccurring errors, managers share accountability at least for the fact that they are the ones who hire (provision), assign work to (organize), and support poorly performing direct reports. In other words, managers are the ones placing the direct reports in situations where they are not able to perform well.

Problem solving, together with diagnosis and analysis, are equally important, and are occasionally required to support all management functions at all management levels.

Since it is impossible to avoid problems 100% of the time, the best solution for a manager is the adoption of a preventive approach. This can be achieved through good Planning, Monitoring (including ongoing external environmental scanning), Supporting, and Cultural Modeling.

No problem can be solved from the same level of consciousness that created it.

Albert Einstein

4.1.4 Diagnosis & Analysis

It is relevant to observe that during the life cycle of an organization there are many occasions when the employment of diagnosis[10] and/or analysis[11] in support of management functions should be considered imperative. In this regard, it is good to keep in mind that diagnosis and analysis require lots of individual reflection and/or group consultation.

The terms diagnosis and analysis can be used interchangeably. However, in practical management settings they are used for different purposes and with different methods of application. It is also common for them to be applied in combination.

While diagnosis is more frequently used for major improvements, planning, and problem solving, analysis is particularly employed for monitoring.

The initial focus of diagnosis is the examination of a reality, the identification of its *causes*[12], and its relations with other phenomena that are considered unclear. Analysis, on the other hand, starts by accepting that the understanding of a reality is certain, moving on to study causes and relations only if variations take place. Diagnosis begins with the gathering of a comprehensive collection of data. Then the data must be understood, and improvements must be made to the reality. In some cases, improvements are not sufficient, and a new reality must be created. Analysis, in turn, is performed on data that are regularly captured by systems designed specifically to verify that a reality is functioning as planned. The primary purpose of analysis is to identify relevant oscillations and distortions in the organization's performance, markets, and in society. An example is the analysis of monthly financial statements that requires a manager to delve into data generated by the continuous daily operation of the organization.

Two simple and common methods for analyzing data presented in numeric format are:

1. *Horizontal Analysis* – The examination of variations of a (line) item along a certain period. Such an examination is carried out by utilizing reports that present data collected at different intervals of time, such as monthly, quarterly or yearly. The data is arranged side-by-side and comparisons are made between them. Some examples would be the monthly evolution of revenue and the quarterly evolution of inventory.

2. *Vertical Analysis* – The examination of variations of line items in a report in relation to each other. An example would be the percentage of wages in relation to revenue, or the relation between current assets and current liabilities, which provides the ratio of liquidity of the organization.

Regarding diagnosis, the most common ways used to distinguish facts from suppositions or assumptions are:

- Review of hard data
- Observation
- Individual and/or group interview
- Questionnaire

Because each method has its pros and cons, if possible a diagnosis utilizing these techniques should be carried out in the same sequence as presented above. By reviewing hard data first, one can proceed with some ideas of what to observe. With the knowledge acquired by hard data and observation, one can better prepare for interviews. To complete the process, managers can create one or more questionnaires designed with the knowledge of the information gathered so far. These questionnaires help gauge the comprehensiveness of the issues at hand. In addition, questionnaires can serve as good venues for confidential sharing. That said, managers should be careful to avoid an undue influence of one phase over another.

In short, even though everyone in an organization should at times perform some degree of diagnosis and analysis, the authority granted to managers, combined with the specificities of their work and a privileged point of view, confers upon them distinctive qualifications to utilize these procedures more frequently and methodically than others in the organization do.

4.2 Core Functions

Core functions are those management functions that are most explicitly intertwined with the production of deliverables.

Through Planning, Organizing, Provisioning, and Coordinating, managers can increase the prospects of a correct amalgamation of the individual contributions necessary for the collective production of deliverables. Therefore, the execution of the core functions should be considered the main obligation of managers, and should constantly be kept at the forefront of their concerns.

4.2.1 Planning

Planning[13] is an endeavor that should encompass undertakings such as diagnosing reality, setting objectives, developing a plan to reach those objectives, and defining performance indicators to track progress.

Because most of our enterprises are expected to be continuously advancing systems, it is not desirable to approach organizational undertakings as one-time endeavors and/or in isolation from one another. Consequently, managers should approach Planning with a mentality of progressive cycles where steps like implementation and monitoring complement the process.

Some concepts that deserve special consideration due to their distinguished capacity to influence the formulation of plans, and consequently all other organizational work, are mission, visions, objectives, and policies. Their primary value rests on their potential to assist in guiding and unifying people's efforts. As long as they are fair, they can help focus everybody's mind and heart on the same endeavors. Nevertheless, for these ideas to have an encompassing influence over the whole organization, they need to be correctly utilized, and in the case of some of them, correctly unfolded throughout the organization. Thus, one or more of these concepts should be present in every planning process and plan document.

Of all management functions, Planning is the one that has the most potential for benefiting from direct reports' involvement, especially in periods of great complexity or fast change. A joint planning process also helps strengthen a common, shared sense of purpose.

4.2.1.1 Mission

A mission[14] conveys the purpose for the existence of an organization and should therefore serve as the primary point of reference for all stakeholders, including external ones. Accordingly, it has the greatest potential for equally serving all areas of the organization. If possible, it should be the first unifying idea to be adopted.

For a mission to be useful, an elementary and extremely simple requisite is that all stakeholders should know it by heart. For that to happen, missions must be "concise and clear"[*]. What is the value of a mission if no one remembers it? This point should not be underestimated. It is crucial that a mission be remembered and used by everyone in an organization. When people are not unified around a mission, efforts cannot be aligned.

Another especially useful point every mission should include is an inspiring factor. The more inspiring a mission is, the higher the ideal, the more galvanizing it can be. Above all, missions should be fair. A mission that is intended to benefit some in detriment of others can never be unifying.

Due to its focal point and outreach, a third important factor related to the applicability of missions is that they should be as lasting as possible. In reality, they should be the most stable of all unifying ideas. If possible, a mission should be unchallengeable for as long as the organization exists. There are, of course, instances when major forces prompt the review of a mission. In such cases, by developing a new mission it may be possible for the organization to continue making use of its provisions, even if the original purpose has changed. If this is to happen, the process of developing a new mission must not be taken lightly.

Taking the above points into consideration, an example of a mission for a clothing company named *Elegance* could be *Providing Elegant Clothing*. This means that the qualifications for the company's image, product, service, staff, infrastructure, and so on, should be guided by the idea of refinement and nobility that elegance conveys.

---

[*] If desired, managers can create an attachment further elaborating on the mission and principles.

Still, because there are numerous ways to accomplish a mission, it alone cannot guide people's work. It requires supplementary ideas to help further clarify ideas and unify actions.

4.2.1.2 Visions

Visions[15] follow the mission. They are the next step in the process of unifying and galvanizing people's efforts. They reduce the abundance of options for fulfilling the mission, by providing the first glimpses of what is expected to be attained.

Like mission, which is sometimes mistaken for strategy, and strategy, which is often confused with strategic objective, visions are sometimes confused with objectives. Such a mistake might happen when, for instance, a vision is very specific or an objective very vague. When the distinction between them is unclear, organizations tend to think that they have objectives.

The major difference between vision and objective is that the former usually lacks precision. Nevertheless, what it lacks in precision, it compensates for by appealing to the sense of sight, which can help awaken emotions and thus increase motivation.

Vision accomplishes such a feat by serving as a mental picture of a desired state of the organization or parts of it, such as its formal and informal spheres, or its market position, in the near, intermediate, and/or distant future.

This mental image gives internal stakeholders a point of reference for where they should start channeling their efforts. They start thinking about what work should be carried out or adjusted in order to accomplish the mission. For example, the company Elegance mentioned in Mission has a vision for its intermediate future of a global presence, with refined and well-recognized stores attracting a pleased and faithful clientele, that provides unity of thought.

The vision is vague, in the sense that precise guidance is still necessary to bring it to fruition. Among other things, the locations and number of stores must be defined. Vision should therefore be followed by strategic objective, which makes it more specific, and then by operational objectives, which leave no room for misinterpretations. The creation of objectives, then, leads to unity of action.

4.2.1.3 Objectives

Objectives go beyond visions to provide focus, by describing the targets, where to go, or what needs to be built or attained, in simple and unambiguous ways. Objectives allow no margin for multiple interpretations, and thus, unite people's efforts even further. They do so by focusing on precise characteristics of the targets. Without precision, vague objectives can easily fall into the realm of intentions.

For example, someone who wants to go on vacation might picture him or herself on a tropical beach with white sand and calm, clear blue water, instead of at a ski resort. To create an objective for this vision, the person should precisely identify a beach by location and even name. With an objective in hand, this person can now develop a plan that designates the participants, resources available and/or necessary (like money, transportation, and accommodation) and a timeframe, allowing for the attainment of the objective and the materialization of the vision.

In organizations, targets do not always have such a clear physical format. Identification of targets, for instance, can rarely be based solely on locations and names. A target frequently has to be identified or accompanied by measurable, quantitative and/or qualitative indicators.

An objective can be defined, then, as a precise (quantitative or qualitative) identification of what is expected to be attained, such as, for example, a 30% sales increase within the next year, or a 95% customer satisfaction rate within the next six months. This measurability factor becomes the basis for developing the monitoring system.

A popular acronym used to help formulate objectives is SMART[16] (Specific-Measurable-Attainable-Realistic-Timely). With time, like what happens in the gossip/telephone game where, with each pass around the circle, the original communication is distorted, variations of the original version start to appear. The important point is that some basic ideas should be observed in order to facilitate the formulation of objectives.

The following is one of the many variations of the original acronym:

S – Objectives should be "specific" enough to facilitate unity of understanding

M – Objectives should be "measurable" to allow for assessment of progress

A – Objectives should be "agreeable" so that there is good will on the part of those involved

R – "Resources" (and "personnel") should be available to allow for attainment of Objectives

T – Objectives should be given a time frame to pace efforts towards completion

Like plans that receive different names, objectives too receive names like Strategic Objectives, Corporate Objectives, Business Objectives, and Operational Objectives. Furthermore, inconsistency in the use of the terminology has even led to the utilization of "objectives" for strategies, "targets" for operation, and "goals" for budgets.

The company Elegance could have the following objectives:

Strategic Objective

Expand global presence in the next two years by opening one new store in Asia and another in Europe.

Operational Objectives

a. First year

- Acquire properties in Hong-Kong and Paris within the first three months (tough job!)
- Complete architectural plans before July
- Initiate advertisement planning by June
- Initiate construction/refurbishing of stores before October
- Initiate advertisement campaigns by October

b. Second year

- Initiate provisioning processes for each store in January
- Initiate new advertisement planning by March
- Complete construction of stores by May
- Initiate new advertising campaigns two weeks before inaugurations
- Inaugurate stores in June

4.2.1.4 Plans

The focal point of planning is, of course, the plan. A plan is a presentation of the work that needs to be done. It should show how different components with assigned functions and values come together in a dynamic way to attain a purpose that can be expressed as a mission, a vision, or more precisely as an objective. In other words, a plan is a presentation of how humans and resources come together in an organized way to enable defined processes to accomplish a purpose.

As such, plans should present[*] the following:

- Work, such as tasks and activities that should be performed along a timeline to produce the intended deliverable(s)
- Required personnel and resources necessary to implement the work
- Assignment of the pattern of functions and values to personnel and resources
- How personnel and resources should be matched
- Processes
- How the work is to be provisioned

Plans (and planning) can address different work domains and should be developed at every management level for all types of work, from formal to informal.

With such a range of application, plans do not have a single format or correct way to be laid out. Nevertheless, as a way of bringing practicality to the concept, management plans can be categorized into the following three groups, which are employed unequally, depending on the management level:

   a. *Broad plans* – Plans intended to address the needs of a whole organization or large parts thereof over a long period. Compared to other types of plans, broad plans require more groundwork before actual plan formulation, and are primarily developed by top-level and mid-level managers. Some examples are Organizational Strategic Plans, Business Plans, and large-scale Strategic Change Plans.

---

[*] Presentations are more or less detailed, depending on the type of plan.

b. *Restricted plans* – Plans that address issues normally limited to one or a few work areas, such as activities and functional areas. Mid-level and lower-level managers normally employ them. Some examples are Advertising and Promotion Plans, Contingency Plans, Production Plans, Staffing (Personnel) Plans, Small and Medium-scale Strategic Change Plans, and Training and Development Plans.

c. *Action plans* – Plans that emphasize the presentation of sequential actions, such as tasks, small activities, and eventually an overview of larger activities. Lower and mid-level managers are the ones who most often use action plans. Perhaps because their applications are so varied, there are no particular names for action plans.

Action Plan

An action plan, as introduced before, is a list of sequentially correlated or linked actions/tasks and/or activities presented throughout a timeline, with a clear indication of who is responsible for what. Sometimes action plans can present other information, like instructions, necessary resources, and support persons.

A useful way to present action plans is through the utilization of Gantt chart as in the following example:

Budget Calendar

RESPONSIBLE	ACTION	Oct 1	Oct 2-9	Oct 10-15	Oct 16	Oct 17-31	Nov 5	Nov 15	Nov 20	Dec 8	Dec 19	Dec 20
Board	1. Distributes strategic plan											
Budget Committee	2. Prepares financial goals for departments and sends to Board											
Board	3. Approves goals and sends them to Controller's Office											
Controller's Office	4. Distributes budget forms with goals to departments											
Departments	5. Send proposed budgets to Controller's Office for review and consolidation											
Controller's Office	6.Sends any budget that needs correction back to responsible department											
Departments	7. Return revised budgets to Controller's Office											
Controller's Office	8. Completes consolidation of budgets and sends individual and consolidated budgets to the Budget Committee for analysis											
Budget Committee	9. Completes analysis of budgets, if necessary in consultation with departments; sends budgets to Board											
Board	10. Adjusts budgets with Budget Committee, if necessary; sends approved budgets to Controller's Office											
Controller's Office	11. Issues approved budgets											

Table 4.2.1.a

Notes:
- Fiscal Year goes from Jan. 1 until Dec. 31.
- Before preparing budgets, departments should create operational plans using word composition.

Plan Document (Outline)

Actual plan documents end up presenting most elements of a planning process, not just the plan. Such a document should be a manager's first deliverable.

Although it may not be possible to have a universal plan document template, perhaps a basic model could be:

- Executive summary (if applicable)
- Situational analysis
- Statement of objective(s) (and sometimes also presentation of the mission and the vision)
- Plan – Presentation of work along a timeline necessary to reach objectives
    - Presentation of organization of work
    - Presentation of provisions with their assigned functions and values
        - Personnel
        - Resources, such as technology, equipment, and finances
    - Presentation of process(es)
    - Description of deliverable(s) with a specified value
    - How the work is to be provisioned
- Financial statements (plan in financial language)
- Discussion of assumptions (if applicable)
- Annexes

4.2.1.5 Policies

Some people dislike policies because they think that policies[17] constrain initiative and creativity. Policies should orient, not constrain, decision-making and action. They should serve as guideposts—as lighthouses, steering a diversity of minds in the same direction. Well-written policies should provide guidance by delimiting, not eliminating, the range of options. Perhaps policies may be looked at as the warp threads of a carpet around which yarns are woven to form an infinite diversity of patterns.

An example of a policy for the company Elegance could be "associates' clothing should be dignified". Such a policy addresses the image issue directly related to the mission, while still allowing for sensibility and flexibility to changes in culture, location, climate, events, fashion, technology, and so forth.

The main purpose of policies is to guide and secure the organizational alignment. This alignment is sought by trying to ensure adherence to the mission and strategies, in particular. As a result, policies are deliverables that only top management should produce.

The creation or revision of policies should be one of the first pieces of conceptual work carried out by top-level managers after the completion of the strategic planning phase. This timing is important because policy statements, added as attachments to the strategic plan document, will assist with the unfolding process by being available at the beginning of each subsequent management level's planning processes.

One of the implications is that policies should have long life spans, particularly those that are directly associated with the mission. Still, they are not meant to last forever, and as such, can be revised. There will always be times, even in the middle of operational cycles, when one needs to review policies that have become outdated and restrictive to advancement. In any case, the revision of policies should not be taken lightly. Specific processes should be put into place for initiating and carrying out policy changes in the middle of a cycle, since policies are far-reaching, and changes can lead to unforeseen consequences in different parts of the organization.

Policies, together with other instruments, such as norms and guidelines, fall under the group of decisions referred to as *normative*—decisions that establish standards. Another set of instruments, referred to as *mandates*, provides details about the application of normative decisions. Mandates include rules, regulations, instructions, and so on. Both groups of decisions should be part of the administrative manual.

The degree to which normative decisions and mandates are employed depends on the management levels. While normative decisions tend to convey principles and are usually used by higher management levels, mandates are often situationally based and are usually used by lower management.

These two groups of decisions should not be confused with each other. While normative decisions should allow some freedom, mandates, on the other hand, are used for situations where there is very little or no opportunity for choice or discussion. Although decisions should be strictly followed, mandates should allow for easy modification. The contexts where mandates are adopted are more changeable, requiring decisions intended for shorter periods and issued in much larger numbers.

By consciously linking mission, visions, objectives, plans, policies, and other decision instruments, managers take a major step toward creating alignment throughout the organization.

Quick Overview of Main Deliverables of Planning Function

Planning Function's Main Deliverables	Description
Mission	"Concise" statement about the organization's existential purpose.
Visions	Imaginary pictures of a future state of the organization, or parts thereof, used to unify understanding and motivate as to fulfill mission.
Objectives	Intermediary and final aims for strategies, operations, projects, and so on, expressed in a precise quantifiable manner.
Plans	Description of the work that needs to be done—"how" the mission, objectives, and visions are to be accomplished.
Plan Document	Final deliverable of the planning phase. In addition to the plan (also in budget formats), the document includes other elements such as environmental analysis, mission, visions, and objectives.
Policy (attachment to plan document)	Guidepost for general decision-making. Important element in the creation and maintenance of organizational alignment.

Table 4.2.1.b

Quick Overview of Planning Function by Management Level

Management Level	Planning Function
Top	Determination of mission, creation of long and mid-term visions, setting of (corporate) strategic objectives, design of broad plans, and definition of policies for the entire organization.
Middle	Creation of mid- and short-term visions, setting of (business unit) strategic objectives, design of broad and restricted plans, and definition of norms and mandates for major parts of the organization using (corporate) strategic plan document as reference.
Lower	Creation of short-term visions, setting of operational objectives, design of restricted and action plans, and definition of mandates for functional and smaller parts of the organization, based on plan documents created by higher management levels.

Table 4.2.1.c

4.2.2 Organizing

Organizing[18] is the theoretical endeavor of detailing the work that needs to be done and arranging the diverse work units so that they collaborate and complement each other in the production of collective deliverables. Consequently, Organizing should determine the profile of who will be doing what, and with which resources.

Since a system requires that elements be organized in a structure that permits processes to occur, the creation of an organization involves more than positioning work areas in an orderly, but disconnected, manner. It is necessary to consider a holistic arrangement that accounts for the eventual flow of deliverables in order to allow processes to take place. This means that each work area has to be arranged in relation to other internal and external work areas and agents, and lines of connections respecting hierarchy must be drawn between them to indicate where transfers should happen. In other words, Organizing can also be defined as the endeavor of arranging diverse transformational (and intermediation) phases of a process or processes in a structure that permits their integration, enabling the creation of whole, systematized, organic structures.

In general, when we think of organizing things, our first impulse is to arrange objects in a tidy manner. This intuitive approach is also aligned with our reading of the formation of natural systems. As we observe in nature, when a system is formed, distinct elements must first be present. These elements must then come together to create a particular structure. Finally, processes must occur in order for exchanges between the parts to take place. Again, the human body is a perfect example. Different organs are arranged in a human body structure, and exchanges between the organs allow for the preservation of the system.

If the same approach to organizing were adopted in organizational settings, the sequence for carrying out the core management functions would be:

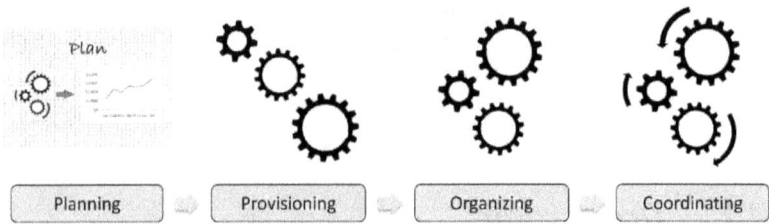

| Planning | Provisioning | Organizing | Coordinating |

Figure 4.2.2.a: Intuitive Approach to Organizing

However, in management, good sense calls for the execution of (theoretical) Organizing before personnel is hired or resources acquired. For that reason, for instance, a job description should be designed first, and only then should a person be invited to occupy the position.

The right sequence for executing the core management functions should be:

| Planning | Organizing | Provisioning | Coordinating |

Figure 4.2.2.b: Appropriate Approach to Organizing

Accordingly, top management should take the first step in the Organizing endeavor, by (broadly) departmentalizing the necessary work beyond what has already been specified in the plan. This is done by theoretically arranging the work in a chart that portrays the organizational structure. At this stage, the structure often presents only larger areas, such as business units and/or functional areas, and possibly key external agents. Top-level management should accomplish this first phase of the Organizing effort after the strategic planning phase, and it should be one of top management's main Organizing deliverables.

Top management continues the process by further defining and detailing some of the work that needs to be executed and pointing out the necessary provisions that will be required for its implementation. The process then cascades throughout the organization—that is, the departmentalization endeavor continues all the way down preferably with different management levels contributing to it.

An issue that deserves special consideration is the common misunderstanding regarding the effectiveness of some very important organizing tools. Many managers do not want to consider certain tools because they feel that the pace of change is so fast that what these tools help organize quickly becomes irrelevant. Interestingly enough, one of the reasons for this disconnect between what was organized and the present reality is precisely a lack of organization, which is at the beginning and not the end of changing processes. Without organization, there is no stability, and with instability, there is uncontrolled change.

A classical example of such a disconnect is the job description, which, though often only seen as a training tool, is actually first and foremost a very important instrument required to organize individual work. If direct reports' duties are changing too fast, it is probably because managers are constantly reassigning new work, and not because direct reports just feel like doing something else. Similarly, if managers' job descriptions are not keeping pace with reality, it is probably because managers are not retaining a good handle on the operations. In summary, if managers keep assigning new work to their direct reports, job descriptions will always be inaccurate.

Such situations raise questions like:

- Are these managers considering the impact of their changes on what has been planned?
- Are they creating new plans as fast as they are assigning new work?
- Are there even plans in place?

On the other hand, in an ever-evolving organic structure, managers have to periodically reorganize work, keeping in mind that the pace of change should be different at different management levels. Top management organizes with the intention that things will be stable for a significant period, and when changes come, they are usually more drastic and far-reaching than what occurs at other levels. At the other extreme, lower management should be prepared to live with much shorter, albeit also planned, intervals of change, which should be incremental and less drastic.

How to organize also depends on what is being organized. For example, some organizing endeavors, like a factory floor plan, might require the assistance of specialists. Other organizing efforts might be delegated to non-manager direct reports, like file storage, small databases, and small inventories. Whatever the case may be, managers should have some level of expertise related to the organization that needs to take place in their area of responsibility.

Some common tools that managers have at their disposal for organizing are:

- Agenda
- Database
- Distributive Table of Labor
- File
- Flowchart
- Job Description
- Manuals
- Maps
    - Factory Floor Plan
    - Layout
- Organizational Chart
- Schedule

Quick Overview of Organizing Function by Management Level

Management Level	Organizing Function
Top	Theoretically defines the largest areas of the organization through the endeavor of departmentalization, creating the top part of the organizational structure. Determines additional important deliverables and work that need to be generated beyond what has already been specified in the plan. Indicates and assigns functions and values to key supplementary provisions to be obtained. Organized things should be stable for a significant period.
Middle	Advances the endeavor of departmentalization for specific large area(s) of the organization, such as functional areas. Determines additional deliverables and work that need to be generated beyond what has already been specified in the plan. Indicates and assigns values and functions to supplementary provisions to be obtained. Organized things should be stable for a moderate period.
Lower	Advances the endeavor of departmentalization for smaller areas of the organization. Determines building block deliverables and work to be carried out. Assigns functions and values to building block provisions. Reorganization should be reasonably frequent and incremental.

Table 4.2.2

4.2.3 Provisioning

Provisioning is the practice of identifying and obtaining all tangible and intangible elements necessary to generate the work required to produce the desired deliverables, and placing them in accordance with the arrangements previously made in the plan and expanded during Organizing. Provisioning includes personnel and all necessary resources, like initial capital, working capital, knowledge, information, technologies, raw materials, energy, infrastructure, equipment, tools, contracts, business licenses, and brands.

Most provisions have to be obtained externally, but some have to be developed in-house, like brands, technologies, and knowledge not found elsewhere. In this regard, the development of a computer program for sale is not a resource, but the development of a special computer language or equipment to produce the program is. Hence, a Research and Development (R&D) department, which has the purpose of creating new products, is not a provisioning area. In other words, whatever is created by the organization for the benefit of external agents only may not be considered a resource. In some instances, like with a brand, an element may be both an internal resource and an external deliverable (see "image" type of brand). Organizational culture, which is of consequence to both the organization and external agents, is not a resource, but rather a product of personnel.

Due to the organic nature of organizations, and to some extent organizations created for projects as well, Provisioning cannot be approached as a one-time job. As a management function, it should not be placed in the back of a manager's mind after a startup or after the initial periods of a fiscal year. An organization is a system that can be compared to a living body, which requires continuous feeding and attention. Personnel suffers turnovers, raw materials have to be continuously flowing in, some assets depreciate, knowledge is constantly advancing, technology becomes obsolete, societal realities are incessantly evolving, and new financial resources are always required.

Managers should also be alert when new or renewed provisions are introduced into the organization, since they have the potential to trigger significant change. A very simple example of this is the upgrading of a computer program.

Another important thing that managers need to be conscious of is that different types of provisions during different conditions and phases of the organizational life cycle usually require specific identifying and obtaining processes. Associates, for instance, might be invited to join the organization during its initial stages without following rigorous procedures, but the same should not occur at advanced stages.

As is the case with all other management functions, the function of Provisioning is also carried out with variations in accordance with management levels. However, regardless of management level, while Planning lends itself to good direct report involvement, Provisioning is perhaps better suited to being delegated to direct reports or outsourced. Maybe that is why it is common practice for managers to pass on to direct reports a great portion of the daily Provisioning work, especially when it is not related to costly resources, and then to be involved mainly at certain key steps through internal control systems. Once operations are underway, managers only need to engage fully in this function when crucial provisions are considered to be at stake.

Quick Overview of Provisioning Function by Management Level

Management Level	Provisioning Function
Top	Obtains external provisions, especially noteworthy financial sums. Obtains key personnel and technology. Spearheads the in-house development of some provisions, like the brand. Transfers financial resources to middle management to be disbursed in accordance with plan requirements. Since all hiring and termination of personnel have to be signed off by a "registered agent" with the legal power to do so, top-level managers are generally involved at all levels with this element of provisioning.
Middle	Obtains especially costly tangible and intangible provisions, like infrastructure, staff, and equipment, externally and/or develops them in-house. Secures the regular acquisition of key provisions, like raw materials. Makes resources, especially financial ones, available to lower-level management, primarily for obtaining non-financial current assets.
Lower	Works with middle management to obtain external provisions, especially non-financial current assets, which are to be deployed directly into the production system. Occasionally develops provisions in-house.

Table 4.2.3

4.2.4 Coordinating

Once Planning, Organizing, and Provisioning are complete, it is time to integrate everything*, to give life to the structure and turn it into a "living" system.

---

* Again, this initial description of the life of an organization is intended to facilitate the understanding of how functions relate to one another at a single management level. In practice, during ongoing operation, the execution of these functions in relation to each other at different management levels follows an interwoven, rather than a sequential, pattern.

Thus, Coordinating[19] is the practice of creating the conditions to allow for a smooth, well-ordered flow of deliverables created by different work areas inside an organization, and between the organization and external systems. Because Coordinating is associated with the transfer phase of a process, while carrying out this function managers should occupy themselves with the integration of work areas, and not with the transformation that takes place at individual workstations.

The function of Coordinating addresses issues like frequency, timing, speed, and volume of the deliverables. Attention also needs to be devoted to the medium used to allow the transfer of the deliverables to take place, such as forms, computer connections, conveyor belts, and even humans. In this regard, managers need to address matters such as substance, format, capacity, and size. Furthermore, attention must also be dedicated to keeping mediums clean from possible interference that can affect the deliverables' integrity while they are transiting between work areas. Remember: *garbage in, garbage out!*

Even if a manager has just one or no direct reports at all, this notion of integration still applies. In the case of one direct report, there are still connections with other areas, with external agents, and between the direct report and the manager. And in the case of a "manager" (one-person business) that has to handle several distinct work areas without direct reports, he or she still has to watch the flow of deliverables between those areas and with external agents.

Because no one has the capacity to oversee the transfer of multiple deliverables simultaneously, managers should establish the flow of transfers, and not be the delivery person. Managers should not normally participate directly in the transferring of deliverables when it is the responsibility of their direct reports. In fact, there are even situations when workstations should handle their own transfer issues directly with each other.

Like the previous core functions of Planning, Organizing and Provisioning, Coordinating should be periodic. Once transfer issues are defined and deliverables are flowing, the function should, in theory, take a "break" until adjustments are necessary or opportunities for improvements arise. Perhaps that is why in very well-created systems, managers might be absent for relatively significant periods without having consequential impact on the operations.

Since transfers overseen by lower management levels tend to involve a greater number of workstations handling non-managerial work than at higher levels, their definitions require more attention. Concomitantly, these transfers should be more rigorously respected. As a result, at lower management levels, changes to transfer definitions should be approached more formally. Most changes, after careful analysis, should lead only to small adjustments, while, after thorough diagnosis, overall process redesigns should preferably come as a consequence of new plans. If small adjustments are not regularly made, then managers should expect to face the consequences of performing major corrections without adequate time for planning.

In top-level management, transfers occur primarily in the interpersonal work domain, relaying mostly information and knowledge. This means that fixing transfer issues, such as the format of deliverables, mediums, or timing, usually takes place during one-on-one or group meetings. Hence, transfers at higher management levels can be altered more easily.

Regardless of the management level, however, coordination that happens in the interpersonal work domain can be very rewarding, and sometimes equally challenging.

For instance, on the one hand, assuming that the culture values good behavior, managers that are given sufficient authority can play a key role in facilitating the integration of people, in ways that can lead to happiness and well-being. On the other hand, if an organization has a culture that does not try to promote the existence of healthy social interactions, managers might end up routinely facing conduct that can prove to be extremely disruptive to the system.

It should be noted that conduct does not have to be explicitly aggressive to be upsetting. For example, just by clinging rigidly to their ways of doing things, individuals, often moved by the desire to preserve the status quo, can also be very disruptive to organizational processes. Furthermore, whether resisting change or not, by upsetting processes, unfitting behavior has the potential to cause harmful changes to particular work areas, and even to an organization as a whole.

Undoubtedly, out of all types of integration that coordination has to deal with, interpersonal work stands out. Some reasons might be that:

a. Almost all interpersonal contacts transfer some deliverable, often in the form of information, even though some of these deliverables might not even be beneficial to the duties of those receiving them.

b.   Deliverables related to the formal sphere of the organization transferred solely through direct personal contacts run the risk of not being as complete or accurate as those deliverables transferred through other mediums.

c.   During interpersonal work, the flow, or the way direct reports relay deliverables, can be even more important than the deliverables themselves. The reason for this is that the manner in which individuals communicate with each other is at the heart of human relations, and therefore shapes the way organizations function.

Now, unless a person simultaneously espouses more than one concept of human beings, there is only one right way to communicate. For those who recognize that humans, in essence, are social beings, the foundation of communication includes a language, verbal and corporeal, that is non-threatening, peaceful, and pleasant—a language that is attractive and conducive to association, cooperation, and integration. It definitely cannot be aggressive and conflictive, leading to division.

To the extent that it is impossible for managers to be constantly involved with all transfers related to the area(s) under their responsibility, the continuous intermediation of interpersonal work is completely out of the question. Although Coordinating can influence behavior, this management function is not suitable for addressing all interpersonal issues. In particular, interpersonal problems must be approached wisely through the execution of other management functions, such as Supporting and Cultural Modeling and, above all, through the employment of Consultation. For processes between the organization and external agents, Coordinating should be executed in partnership with external personnel as much as possible.

During the execution of the function of Coordinating,

- Managers should design representations of processes under their responsibility. A flowchart is the main tool for this purpose. For representations under non-manager direct reports' responsibilities, managers should also use standard operating procedures (SOPs).
- Managers should define, alone or with technical assistance, mediums of transfers. In relation to humans as "mediums", beyond

specifying what to communicate (output), managers should also clarify the expected behavior in line with the appropriate norms of social interaction and with the organization's culture.

- Managers should determine, preferably with the involvement of others, the characteristics of the transfers, such as frequency, timing, speed, and volume.
- Managers should define transfer issues in such a way as to best protect mediums from interference that can affect the integrity of deliverables flowing between work areas.

Thus, one of the main duties of management is the job of coordinating the transfer of work between work areas—that is, Coordinating the transfers between successive changes or transformations (and intermediations) as to help bring life to a system.

Quick Overview of Coordinating Function by Management Level

Management Level	Coordinating Function
Top	Coordinates the integration of large work areas, such as business units and functional areas, with each other and with external agents. Often defines transfer issues, with direct reports' involvement. Flow at this level is relatively sparse and mediums are simple. The most frequent elements flowing between work areas are information and knowledge. Most of the time and energy dedicated to this function is spent in meetings.
Middle	Coordinates the internal integration of mid-size work areas such as functional areas and large activities under own work area, and works with peers and external agents to integrate own area with others. Establishes detailed transfers. Dedicates a reasonable amount of time to this function. Some flow at this level is quite frequent and some mediums are somewhat more complex.
Lower	Coordinates the integration of smaller work areas such as activities and tasks under one's own work area and with external areas in partnership with peers and/or external agents. Defines very detailed transfer matters. Flow at this level is fast and mediums tend to be relatively more complex. Frequent adjustments are necessary at this level. More time is dedicated to this function than to others.

Table 4.2.4

4.3 Complementary Functions

Complementary functions are the management functions that must be performed in order to support the production system. In other words, they are not as explicitly intertwined with the production of deliverables as the core functions are, but they play an important role not only in the maintenance of the organization but in its advancement as well. Through complementary functions like Monitoring, Supporting, Cultural Modeling and Liaising, managers ensure a healthy functioning of the system.

Consider, for instance, the relevance of the work done to produce a deliverable that will be used by external agents, and the cleaning work performed in its support. The production work is the organization's reason for being, but without the contribution from the cleaning work, production eventually comes to a halt. Such is the relation between core and complementary functions.

4.3.1 Monitoring

Once the organization is up and running—that is, once Planning, Organizing, Provisioning, and Coordinating have been carried out to keep the organization alive and moving in the right direction—it is essential that the system and its external connections and environment be constantly monitored.

Monitoring[20] is necessary because everything in this physical world, including organizations, is constantly changing, even if it is not perceptible to our senses. In organizations, every element, formal and informal aspect of the system, work domain, and external matter can be subject to monitoring. If changes are not to cause an organization to stray from what has been created, Monitoring must constantly be employed to prompt the other management functions to return the organization to its intended course whenever necessary. For the most part, a manager can accomplish this by adopting one of the following approaches:

a) Driving things back to the way they were before the deviation took place

b) Introducing new advancements into the system

Contrary to the core functions, once the system is functioning, Monitoring has to be uninterrupted. If all core functions have been well executed, Monitoring should occupy a significant portion of managers' time. Even though some may think this function is of secondary importance, its value should not be underestimated. Once the organization is operating, managers might have a hard time performing other management functions well without first being prompted by and fed with the input gathered from Monitoring.

Coordinating, in particular, can greatly benefit from Monitoring. Coordinating without a clear understanding of what is taking place can well be a recipe for chaos. For instance, how is it possible to adjust the frequency, speed, and timing of flow, the format, size, and capacity of mediums, and the deliverable specifications without data gathered from monitoring? At least it would require constant diagnoses. Managers can only seriously adjust transfers, reshuffle the priorities of deliverables, and assign new tasks if they have a good picture of what is happening. Without a clear image of what is going on, managers might as well restart their work from scratch as if the organization has just been created.

That said, no organization has the capacity to monitor everything, so cost/benefit considerations are frequently adopted in guiding managers on what to monitor. Besides, such considerations vary from organization to organization and from management level to management level. Depending on the provisions available, managers may also delegate parts of this function to specialized direct reports. Regardless, as a way of further increasing the outreach of monitoring, everybody should contribute, with direct reports monitoring their areas, and managers monitoring their own performance.

From a manager's perspective, it would be ideal to continually monitor key provisions, arrangements of and transfers between work areas and with external agents, and key external matters, with the intention of ensuring the maintenance and advancement of the system and keeping it in line with the organization's plans. In practice, unless a manager employs sophisticated tools, preferably application software, the possibility of monitoring a large number of factors will never be more than an aspiration.

A reasonable approach is for managers, individually or on a team, to identify some main elements to track. These may be inferred from the mission and visions, but by design, the large majority of them should be extracted from the objectives established during the planning phases. For example, an objective of a 20% increase in customer satisfaction in the next six months could be tracked by means of the number of complaints, returns, and/or compliments. Negative performance towards reaching such an objective, then, prompts managers to investigate, for instance, if provisions, work arrangement and/or flow are having issues that need to be addressed.

Once a manager specifies what is to be monitored, he or she must set up a system for recording the operation, which includes its deliverables, like particular tasks, activities, or customer complaints. The operation might be recorded, for example, through logs, forms, surveys, and observations, and the data compiled and presented in the form of written reports, tables, graphics, and financial statements.

Physical observations* and verbal reports, although valid, should not be the first choice for monitoring. These alone can rarely cover a sufficient number of events to provide the needed clarity. Additionally, verbal reports might lack precision and might not contribute to the organization's historical records. Still, because of their practicality, they are useful for interim reporting.

By far the best system for recording operations is financial accounting; so much so that in virtually all countries it is the system used by law for recording all aspects of operations that conventionally have financial representation. This system covers so many aspects of the operation and in such detail that it is not only capable of tracking many elements specified in objectives, but it tracks almost entire plans. Furthermore, because it uses the universal language of numbers, it can also consolidate the diverse facets of the organization's undertakings in almost any desired combination, even in single global reports. Accounting achieves this feat by recording everything that comes into the organization, is transformed or created, and goes out of the organization, plus the movement of most of its assets.

Certainly, accounting is not perfect, but without a doubt, it is the broadest of all recording systems, and it can be extremely accurate. Accounting has been perfected throughout the centuries and most of the criticisms leveled against it seem to be more the result of a poor understanding of how

---

* Managerial physical observation should not be confused with non-managerial physical inspections for the purpose of quality control.

to use it than a weakness of the science itself. For example, one could say that accounting cannot capture customer satisfaction. Personal interviews and questionnaires might be required to understand what customers' thoughts are. However, like most other monitoring systems, accounting can provide many important initial indications from data, like the increase, decrease, or steadiness of sales, the number of returns, and seasonality. Furthermore, by using comparisons, accounting can provide some insight into customers' concerns with factors like price, quality, and service.

Whatever the system, as the operation is being recorded, the data should be:

a) Evaluated in relation to mission and visions
b) Measured against objectives and plans, and in the case of accounting, against budgets
c) Analyzed along a timeline
d) Analyzed by comparing portions of the data against one another

By doing so, monitoring can expose deviations in the operation and make deliberations regarding the need for corrections.

If corrections are necessary, managers and/or direct reports must carry them out by employing one or more of the other management functions, and in some instances, following pre-established procedures. For example, one or more of the other functions should address each of the following issues detected by monitoring:

- Strategic plans that are falling short of a changing societal reality.
- Resources that need to be upgraded.
- Personnel that need to be trained.
- Transfers that are no longer suitable to new arrangements and/or deliverable specifications.

Even problems with monitoring itself, like tracking obsolete data and the utilization of outdated tools that can no longer capture an accurate picture of the organization's true performance, should be addressed by tapping into other management functions.

When considering which actions to take, the degree of deviation and the timing to deal with it could be important variables to observe. For instance, if more than halfway through a fiscal year an operational plan is deemed weak, it still might be better to carry out the plan with small adjustments all the way to the end, rather than to try to redo the plan at that point in time. Furthermore, analysis alone may not be enough to reach a clear understanding about the causes of the deviation. In such circumstances, a diagnosis is also required. Indeed, the essence of monitoring is thorough analysis and, when necessary, serious diagnosis.

Another concern when dealing with deviation is the need to strike a balance between maintenance and advancement, between stability and change. The starting point for moving towards such a balance is the understanding that the difference between these concepts is mainly a matter of speed—that is, change and stability can be approached as identical events that occur at a different pace. As implied above, on the one hand, change is a law of nature, a requirement of life, and as such, it cannot be stopped. On the other hand, some level of apparent stability is necessary if humans are to find the conditions to perform well. In the long run, from an organization's perspective, the adoption of a single speed, like very slow (stability) or too fast (constant change) is neither practical nor realistic. Broadly speaking, the dynamic might be:

- Major improvements, or changes, should take place sparsely through planning
- Minor improvements, or maintenance, should be implemented between planning phases
- Minor improvements should be sought primarily through Supporting and Cultural Modeling

Even though monitoring, as a constant accompaniment of operation, is only able to prompt corrections once it detects deviations, it can empower managers to be proactive as well. The truth is that there is no dichotomy between being proactive and reactive. Both have value and appropriate moments for application.

Notwithstanding its importance, many managers unfortunately feel uncomfortable using monitoring when it comes to direct reports and their assignments. Perhaps one of the reasons this happens is because of the aversion that many direct reports have developed from having managers deal with their work in authoritarian or paternalistic ways. However, for fine performance, it is essential that managers know everything that is going on in their areas of responsibility, including how the direct reports are executing their work. This practice does not mean that direct reports are not entitled to some level of autonomy. This means that there is a general and true recognition that each work area is the result of a collective endeavor. It must become clear that the success and failure of work assigned to direct reports is also dependent on the manager's contributions.

As the saying goes, "what gets measured gets done".

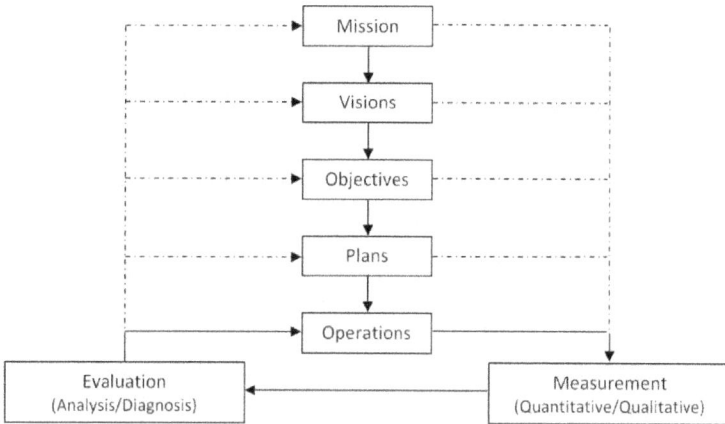

Figure 4.3.1: Monitoring Loop

Personnel Monitoring and Performance Review

Should personnel—that is, managers and non-managers—be monitored? Should managers monitor what their direct reports are doing, or check if they are respecting their daily hours? In theory, it could be argued that personnel should not be monitored, that both managers and direct reports should be able to demonstrate a level of maturity and commitment where such concerns should be nonexistent. Still, because personnel are the "soul" of an organizational system, they also require attention.

Unfortunately, while some aspects of monitoring of personnel might not be that difficult, when human emotions come into the mix, monitoring can become very tricky. Some managers attempt to sidestep people's sensibilities, by trying to dissociate the human element from the associate's performance and deliverables. The intention is to focus primarily on the deliverables and less on the performance, leaving the "person" out of the equation as much as possible. Although in many instances this approach may generate reasonable results, at its foundation it is probably as unrealistic as the idea of dissociating task and process.

A great solution to the monitoring of personnel that can simultaneously address the human element, performance and deliverables is the creation of a culture of collective learning, where monitoring is carried out in a context of continual individual and collective striving for improvement and excellence. In such a culture, a desire for constant reexamination, for a constant analysis of an ever-evolving reality, becomes installed as the norm. It becomes the new way of being.

On the other hand, performance review[21] of personnel, which unfortunately seems to be necessary for the purpose of promotion and rewards, is almost certainly the most difficult thing to do in an organization, and therefore cannot be based solely on data gathered from a monitoring system.

Some of the reasons for this difficulty are as follows:

a. The relation between an individual with his or her manager, direct reports, and other internal and external work areas is organic.

b. The level of provisions available to an individual has a direct impact on his or her performance.

c. Individuals can have issues that might affect the review process – personal baggage, such as affection and bias; inaccuracies of interpretation; and memory lapses.

It follows that, to a certain degree, an individual's performance is dependent on the resources available and on the performance of others, particularly on the performance of his or her manager and of those directly adjacent in a given process.

For a fair review of an individual performance, then, at least in theory, a review system would have to be based on a complex formula that would take into consideration the weighted relevance of some positive factors, and discount the possible negative influence of others, such as:

- The performance of the individual being reviewed, in both the formal and informal spheres of the organization
- The work group or unit of the individual being reviewed
- His or her manager or direct reports
- The provisions available
- The upper management
- The other internal and external work areas and external agents

With or without the use of complex formulas, everybody should at least know ahead of time how and by whom their performance is going to be reviewed. If possible, they should even be allowed to participate in the creation of the review system. Additionally, particular attention should be paid to the fact that the system must take into consideration concrete, measurable facts. In the end, it is best to perform reviews as collectively as possible, allowing for the participation of external agents.

Perhaps one day this complex issue of performance review will decrease in importance. Still, it will probably never be eliminated, as individuality and differentiation will always allow for and require the identification of individual contributions for which one should receive his or her due.

Quick Overview of Monitoring Function by Management Level (not taking into consideration direct report monitoring)

Management Level	Monitoring Function
Top	Especially concerned with long- and mid-term performance. Monitoring is carried out primarily through written and verbal reports with sporadic physical examinations. Macro indicators are tracked through financial reports, sales volume, headcount, and so forth, for monthly, quarterly and annual operations.
Middle	Especially concerned with mid- and short-term performance. Monitoring is based on weekly and monthly performance, and is carried out primarily through written and verbal reports, and some physical examination.
Lower	Especially concerned with short-term performance. Daily monitoring of operation is primarily carried out through statistical measurements and physical examination of samples.

Table 4.3.1

4.3.2 Supporting

Supporting[22] is the practice whereby managers assist the direct reports and others to create the conditions where they can perform their work at their best, and therefore contribute to the establishment of individual and collective well-being. One thing that Supporting should not be confused with is Provisioning, through which a manager also considers the necessary direct and indirect tools, materials, and technology that their direct reports need for their work.

Although Supporting is exclusively related to personnel, there is little value in spending energy trying to psychologically analyze direct reports. Instead, managers should concentrate on creating fair work environments where the channels of communication are always open and transparent—environments where there is no need for hidden agendas and where people are free to appropriately express themselves. When executing the Supporting function, managers should be careful not to patronize their direct reports, nor to treat them in a condescending manner. The basis for Supporting is not the idea that direct reports need assistance because they are less knowledgeable or less capable.

Support from managers is particularly useful because they are positioned outside the spheres of transformation and transfer in relation to direct reports who are non-managers, and outside the span of direct management in relation to managers who are direct reports. As such, managers can add a perspective that those directly involved with certain undertakings usually cannot. In addition, especially those engaged with non-managerial work generally do not have the luxury of time to stop their work to look for ways of improving it or to help others to do so.

Managers can figure out what is missing, what can be improved upon formally and informally, and can come up with options for how to assist their direct reports. Even so, they should ideally first approach the direct reports without preconceived ideas. Managers should ask the direct reports and others how they can be of help—listen to them, learn what they feel they need, and determine in consultation what types of support they would like to receive. In this regard, it is important to point out that such an approach requires a certain degree of altruism from managers, a posture of service, and continued accompaniment of and engagement with their direct reports.

In line with human complexity, managers can provide support in a variety of ways—intellectual, emotional, and material. In any case, it is helpful to think of these efforts as being either inner or outer support for direct reports.

In the case of outer support, managers can look at a variety of ways to provide the necessary formal backing that their direct reports can use to facilitate their work. For example, managers can:

- Help the direct reports balance their work and non-work matters
- Provide indirect benefits, sometimes by tapping into Provisioning
- Provide support in company and out of company
- Provide extra training for ongoing operations (for new processes, training should be considered Provisioning)
- Assist with the solution of problems
- Occasionally contribute to the performance of tasks, like assisting with an audit preparation that is running late or a physical rearrangement of office furniture

In the case of inner assistance, again, managers are not psychologists. Hence, the effort is better directed towards empowering direct reports to handle their own issues, and assume control over their own development—that is, "take ownership" of their duties, and ultimately, have the same posture towards the whole enterprise. In this connection, managers can use coaching as long as it is carried out with the right spirit.

Managers primarily empower direct reports by permitting them to make decisions individually and in groups. This implies that direct reports are granted a margin of error within which to operate. Furthermore, not every deliverable that turns out to be different from what was expected is necessarily wrong. In many cases, managers should just relax, accept the direct report's contribution, and move on to focus on things that only he or she can do.

The freedom to make decisions is a powerful motivator. It opens the door to individual initiative and creativity, reducing the need for support from management. The opposite is also true. There are few things managers can do that are as disempowering to direct reports as removing their capacity to make decisions about their sphere or responsibility. If direct reports take control of their own progress, virtually the only inner support needed from managers is the job of encouraging their direct reports. However, no one should assume that this is an easy undertaking. The art of encouraging can be a tricky one. It requires qualities like sensibility, sincerity, moderation, and wisdom. Encouraging should not be reduced to indiscriminate praising. Repetitively telling people how good they are might end up just boosting their egos. Rather than only praising a person, it might be helpful to highlight results, to point out the general contributions the direct reports are making to the whole. Moreover, encouragement is not the same as trying to motivate by offering incentives, which can easily slip into manipulation.

Incentives should not be confused with justifiable compensation for individual superior performance. In this regard, individual compensation must be approached with concern for the organization as a whole; otherwise, it can become unfair to the group. Superior performance should be the result of a personal drive for excellence.

The above points, combined with the fact that the execution of Supporting is relatively less constrained by plans* than many of the other functions, makes it easy to use Supporting in a way that is proactive. The relative freedom from plans adds to the manager's capacity for contributing ideas that are "outside-the-box". Being proactive goes a long way toward positioning work ahead of the curve, improving performance, beating targets, and advancing the organization.

A positive implication of the correct execution of the Supporting function is the elimination of a function like Commanding. It is not possible for Supporting and Commanding functions to be simultaneously applicable. They are opposing philosophies of life, attitude, and work.

Quick Overview of Supporting Function by Management Level

Management Level	Supporting Function
Top	Provides primarily inner support with an attitude of service.
Middle	Provides a mixture of inner and outer support with an attitude of service.
Lower	Provides a mixture of inner and outer support with some emphasis on outer. Support is primarily concerned with the execution of tasks and activities. Maintains an attitude of service, "doing it together".

Table 4.3.2

---

* Proactivity does not imply skipping Planning. Although a great deal of the Supporting effort is dedicated to unforeseen circumstances that arise from day-to-day operation, supporting endeavors can and should also be planned.

4.3.3 Cultural Modeling

Cultural Modeling[23] is about systematically making a conscious and positive effect on the informal sphere of the organization. However, before carrying out the function of Cultural Modeling, managers must revisit their personal philosophy of life and of human beings. This is important because management needs to be clear about how to harmonize the role played by top managers in shaping an organizational culture, especially in the absence of a philosophy of consultation and the notion that an organizational culture is the sum of all members' expressions resulting from a dynamic between the individuals and the environment.

Regardless of how an organizational culture should be shaped, the rationale that backs management in executing the function of Cultural Modeling is grounded in the authority and specific role that it has to play.

Equipped with as deep an understanding of human nature as possible, managers can consciously labor, hopefully with collective involvement, to systematically promote a culture that is relevant to the organization's mission and strategy. It is important to observe that Cultural Modeling has nothing to do with trying to interfere with people's individualities.

In moving forward with the process of promoting an organizational culture, it can be helpful to keep in mind three of its aspects as categorized below:

1. *Core values of an organization* – Even if not explicitly presented as such, the core values of an organization are a collection of what its people understand to be the fundamental principles that should govern human behavior. Consequently, core values establish the vital rules of engagement—of interactions between the individuals within an organization and with external agents. Human qualities that represent positive core values include truthfulness, fairness, trust, cooperation, and service. Some negative qualities are falsehood, unfairness, dishonesty, and selfishness. Positive qualities are integrating forces, while the negative ones are disintegrating. Core values can be the same for any organization.

2. *Idiosyncrasies of an industry* – Every organization contributes directly to the idiosyncrasies of a particular industry, or the field in which it operates, and at the same time is itself influenced by these same

idiosyncrasies. As a result, some aspects of an organization's culture are in one way or another molded to fit its specific environment. For example, amusement parks and protection service organizations each develop very specific cultural idiosyncrasies suitable to their respective industries of entertainment (merry and casual) and security (serious and disciplined.)

3. *Idiosyncrasies of an organization* – Each organization develops a unique set of cultural idiosyncrasies that other organizations cannot replicate. Such idiosyncrasies emerge because of the combination of the personalities, aptitudes, and interests of those involved with the enterprise. These factors, in turn, are major forces driving an organization's decision-making process, and affect its choices of strategy, structure, orientation towards people, method of operation, and so forth.

Cultural Modeling requires managers to consciously labor to keep culture aligned with mission and strategy by:

a.   Promoting the organization's core values.
b.   Promoting good industry and organizational idiosyncrasies.
c.   Curbing behaviors contrary to the organization's core values.
d.   Suppressing unsuitable industry and organizational idiosyncrasies.

The first steps in Cultural Modeling, then, are the selection of the organization's core values and the qualities that manifest them. This is followed by the identification of the industry's idiosyncrasies that are considered worthy of adopting.

Once managers have decided which culture to foster, they must wisely design and implement a system of rewards and penalties. It should be emphasized that the design of such a system should not begin without a clear understanding of the desired culture. Additionally, it is worth remembering that rewards and penalties are standard features in organizations, even if not formally institutionalized. This means that if the reward and penalty system has not been formally created, it should be reviewed and formalized in light of the desired culture.

Beyond that, Cultural Modeling has to be considered in connection with other management functions, like Organizing, Provisioning, Coordinating, and Supporting, and in connection with a manager's personal example, like his or her behavior and problem-solving style. Intentionally or not, managers do have the potential to significantly affect a culture, and should therefore pursue such influence in a conscious way.

Organizational culture, like everything else that concerns management, should be methodically addressed. If left without systematic attention, single changes like a new member, especially at the top management level, are enough to be a considerably disruptive force, creating constant distractions and eventual conflicts, and ultimately forcing an organization to spend substantial energy trying to readjust its operations. At times, such unplanned changes can even completely reshape an organization's culture, oftentimes sealing its future in a negative way. It is encouraging to note that if an organization's culture is carefully nurtured, those who do not fit eventually leave before having the opportunity to create havoc.

Quick Overview of Cultural Modeling Function by Management Level

Management Level	Cultural Modeling
Top	Selection of organization's core values and promotion of the qualities that manifest them. Selection and promotion of desired key organization idiosyncrasies. Identification and promotion of good industry idiosyncrasies. Curbing of behavior contrary to organization's core values and suppression of unsuitable industry and organizational idiosyncrasies.
	Cultural modeling through strategy, policies, organizational structure, key provisions, supporting, personal example, and creation and enforcement of general reward and penalty system.
Middle	Promotion of core values and qualities that manifest them, and promotion of good industry and organizational idiosyncrasies. Curbing of behavior contrary to core values and suppression of unsuitable industry and organizational idiosyncrasies. Selection and promotion of good business unit and/or functional area idiosyncrasies and curbing of unsuitable ones.
	Cultural modeling through the utilization of policies and a general reward and penalty system, the creation and enforcement of norms related to functional areas, major provisions, processes, supporting, and personal example.
Lower	Promotion of core values and qualities that manifest them, and promotion of good industry and organizational idiosyncrasies. Curbing of behavior contrary to core values and suppression of unsuitable industry and organizational idiosyncrasies. Promotion of good business unit and/or functional area idiosyncrasies, and curbing of unsuitable ones.
	Cultural modeling through the utilization of policies and norms, general and functional area reward/penalty system, processes, supporting, personal example, creation of mandates for specific work areas.

Table 4.3.3

4.3.4 Liaising

The management function of Liaising is the practice of facilitating a general understanding among stakeholders, with the primary intention of increasing universal cohesion.

Inside the organization, managers carry out Liaising by unofficially sharing information, and informally exploring certain issues. It helps keep the different agents abreast of what is happening in other areas, with the organization as a whole, and within the larger societal environment. In some cases, Liaising can also assist with smoothing and bridging of communication. Furthermore, once consultation is institutionalized, Liaising can also serve as an additional means for increasing general participation in management.

Such sharing can give direct reports a broader picture, which in turn can increase their confidence in and commitment to the enterprise. In particular, it should help increase the perception of distributive and procedural justice and further assist areas to stay in sync with the rest of the organization. It can also help reassure direct reports of upper level management's commitment to ongoing plans as well as assist with preparations for possible future changes. In the end, Liaising helps increase the sense of belonging to and participation in the overall execution of an organization's mission, allowing for enjoyment of collective successes.

To carry out the function of Liaising, managers can establish formal times for sharing information with their direct reports and with external stakeholders (when applicable). The information, depending on the direction shared, can address, for instance, the status of one's area, other areas, and/or of the organization's overall progress, pointing out successes and challenges, as well as bringing news from the outside into the organization. On such occasions, the work group can take the opportunity to discuss specific matters in order to deepen understanding.

The management function of Liaising should not be confused with Coordinating. While Coordinating is concerned with the transfer of deliverables in a process, information shared (delivered) during Liaising is not to be used for transformation.

The intermediation of issues and problems of processes with other areas on behalf of or with direct reports is not Liaising. It is Supporting. Moreover, the management function of Liaising is not the standard practice of serving as the point of contact for communications between work areas. Managers might occasionally do that, but in general, such work should be assigned to non-managers. Indeed, if communications mostly take place through managers, it could have the opposite effect than that of increasing cooperation and integration between different areas. The fact is that almost all direct reports do have, and need to have, some sort of formal direct contact with external areas as well. It is basically impossible for managers to completely isolate their direct reports in an organization, and to do so may be extremely counterproductive.

It is important for areas under a manager not to feel like closed systems. Poor Liaising can create "silos", raising barriers between work areas. It might create even larger problems if the formation of silos is due to a manager's desire to gain power by withholding information. If kept in the dark about other areas, direct reports can feel isolated, become misinformed, and will likely be less productive. They might develop mistrust towards managers, and animosity and rivalry towards other areas. It can certainly contribute to the rise in the feeling of injustice. Isolation and lack of global vision can be, particularly in times of crises, extremely damaging to direct reports' morale. In short, poor Liaising can compromise the unity of an organization.

Managers should try to maintain transparency with all internal and external stakeholders, showing genuine concern for the collective well-being and making it clear that they have no hidden agendas. These practices are conducive to an environment of trust, further promoting a healthy work environment.

Quick Overview of Liaising Function by Management Level

Management Level	Liaising Function
Top	Liaising between organization and external stakeholders, such as partners, suppliers, government, and broad society. Liaising between top governance (board) and middle management.
	Sharing information and assisting with broadening the understanding of how factors such as regulations, world economy, politics, industry, social movements, and environment might be influencing the effectiveness and direction of the organization. Sharing internal information and addressing concerns between top governance and middle management.
Middle	Liaising between own area(s) and top-level management, rest of organization and some external agents.
	Sharing information and assisting with broadening the understanding of how factors such as the performance of other business units and functional areas and government regulations might be influencing the effectiveness of one's area(s). Sharing information and addressing concerns between own area(s) and top-level management, rest of organization and some external agents.
Lower	Liaising between own area and middle management, rest of organization and some external agents, like customers and other organizations' low-level management.
	Sharing information and assisting with broadening the understanding of how factors such as other functional areas, clients, and suppliers might be influencing the work group's effectiveness.

Table 4.3.4

5

Span of Direct Management

The span of direct management[1] can cover one or multiple areas and contain none (one-person business) to many direct reports.

In every work assignment, the scope of the work and the workload are major variables in determining one's performance. One of the particularities of managerial positions compared to non-managerial ones, however, is that it is much more difficult to establish an adequate workload for the former than it is for the latter. Consequently, it is also difficult to establish an appropriate and feasible span of direct management. Besides variations in the number of areas and direct reports, the main reason behind this difficulty is the leeway that managers have in significantly changing their own workload. For example, by altering factors such as direct report involvement, delegation, types of direct reports, and level of formality, a manager can dramatically reduce his or her own workload, and as a result be able to take on a broader span of direct management.

Obviously, as is the case with unreasonable non-managerial workloads, problems can also result from situations with inappropriate spans of direct management and heavy managerial workloads.

If a span of direct management stretches too wide for a manager to handle, this can eventually lead to exclusive reactive behavior, a mode where one is constantly trying to put out fires. Some of the first signs that this may be happening are poor communication, difficulty accessing a manager, and a constant changing of priorities by the manager. Of course, a manager may also operate in reactive mode due to a lack of solid knowledge of management principles.

On the other hand, if a span of direct management is too narrow, chances are that there is too little for the manager to do. Unless such a manager is indifferent to the organization and does not assist with non-managerial work, it is quite possible for him or her to start looking for things to do beyond his or her sphere of primary responsibility. A likely scenario would be the manager meddling with work that is the responsibility of his or her direct reports. This behavior can be particularly disempowering to direct report managers, creating confusion and insecurity for other direct reports further down the line, and eventually leading to conflicts. It is worth noting that disrespect of the hierarchical structure does not occur only because of a manager's excess free time. This problem is especially common for successful entrepreneurs who have not refined their management skills.

Managers should keep the important concept of the span of direct management in mind during departmentalization endeavors, and use it to adjust sporadic fluctuations in their workload, keeping their overall performance at its peak.

5.1 Number of Direct Areas and Direct Reports

In addition to managers' leeway to adjust their workloads, the unending diversity and complexity of organizations make it impossible to establish a precise of correct number of direct areas and direct reports for which managers can be responsible.

Generally, the number of areas and direct reports fluctuate in opposite directions from each other as one moves up and down management levels. For instance, as one moves up, the number of direct and indirect areas under a manager's responsibility increases, and the number of direct reports that the manager is capable of interacting with on a regular basis decreases. This arrangement is regulated by the variety of issues that need to be addressed by a single manager.

As the number of issues increases during ongoing operations, a practical limit is eventually reached where a manager's productivity begins to drop. In other words, at some point the amount of work that a manager can directly handle and help integrate becomes impractical. Facing such a situation, managers tend to introduce a new hierarchical level where fewer direct reports become responsible for fewer of areas. The integration of work now progresses through layers.

For example, instead of a single manager trying to keep track of and facilitate the integration of twenty different activities, having four direct report managers facilitate the integration of five activities each is easier and more productive. Then the top manager facilitates the integration of the four sets (5 + 5 + 5 + 5) of activities by dealing with only four direct reports.

As managers begin to have direct reports responsible for greater numbers of areas, the interactions between them require more and more time to cover more issues. Some of the implications are that in such conditions managers have to begin to consider issues in a less repetitive and detailed manner. The focus of the interactions turns, therefore, to broader relational matters, with more analysis of cause and effect taking place. As such, the work becomes more abstract, conceptual, and the issues discussed become less perceptible to the senses.

Inversely, as management levels descend, direct reports are responsible for fewer areas and more standardized, repetitive work. This allows for interactions of shorter duration, which consequently allows managers to interact more frequently with a greater number of direct reports.

Broadly speaking, for mid-sized organizations, a balanced number for the top executive may be 4 to 6 areas, and an equivalent number of direct reports, reducing the number of areas and increasing the number of direct reports as management level decreases. In any case, the best guideline for the number of areas and direct reports is "moderation".

5.1.1 Team Direct Report

Aside from working with direct reports individually or in work groups, a third possibility is to arrange the direct reports in teams.

To work with teams, it is valuable for managers to possess additional expertise, which might include knowledge of the phases that describe the life cycle of a team[2] as follows:

1. Forming – phase where team members are selected
2. Norming – phase where team members establish basic rules of functioning
3. Performing – phase where the team addresses the issue(s) for which it was created
4. Adjourning – phase where the team is disbanded

Furthermore, proficiency with team-related issues[3] such as the ones listed below can also be a great asset:

- Team composition
- Group decision-making
- Team alignment
  - Team mission
  - Team visions
- Team norms
- Team members' roles and responsibilities
- Team communication
- Team meetings
- Conflict resolution
- Team review
- Team and team members rewards and penalties

When working with teams as direct reports, managers have a couple of ways of doing this:

1. *The manager does not attend team operational meetings:*

   The team functions like an individual non-manager or manager direct report. Such a team without an authority figure is sometimes referred to as a "self-managed team", even though it still has to report to someone or to another team. To manage this type of team, managers can adopt a combination of interactions that range from frequent contacts with a team liaison to sparse meetings with the team as a whole.

2. *The manager can participate in team operational meetings in one of the two ways:*

   a. The manager does not maintain a hierarchical position. In this case, the manager's contributions have the same weight as every other team member.

   b. The manager maintains his or her hierarchical status even in re-lation to the internal affairs of the team, including overruling majority decisions.

Because a significant portion of teamwork happens in the context of group decision-making, the utilization of the decision-making method called Consultation greatly facilitates both team performance and team management. With the help of Consultation, teams can easily progress through the different phases of their life cycles and address issues as the ones mentioned above.

Whatever the type of relationship a manager might have with a team, it should be viewed as a single unit and positioned like an individual in the organizational structure, and managers should continue to carry out all management functions in the same basic way. The extra touch should be the incorporation of the above-mentioned expertise into the management functions where relevant. For instance, the expertise related to the Forming phase of the life cycle of a team should be considered by the management function of Provisioning, while Norming can be addressed by Cultural Modeling, and Performing can be handled through Supporting*.

5.2 Direct Report Involvement

Managers cannot achieve an increase in direct report involvement by in-creasing direct report workload or by stimulating direct repot commitment to the organization. To involve direct reports means to include and engage them specifically in the management of the organization. It means allowing

---

* The team itself also has to perform some management functions at different phases of its life cycle, like organizing during Norming and Performing.

them, especially through group decision-making, to assist managers with the execution of management functions.

It is somewhat equivalent to, but in the reverse orientation of, a manager's participation in a direct report's work assignment. The main difference here is that while managers should avoid getting involved in work that is the responsibility of their direct reports, direct reports, on the other hand, should participate in management as much as possible.

The rationale for direct report involvement is grounded on some of the characteristics of the work of management, like its scope, dynamism, complexity, and level of subjectivity. If not properly handled, any of these characteristics can lead to poor management, which in turn, can even unintentionally generate injustice. As such, direct report involvement is not only helpful, but often of paramount importance. The broader the perspective and the more minds seeking solutions together, the better the results. Thus, managers, direct reports, the organization as a whole, and stakeholders all benefit from participative management.

5.3 Delegation

The term delegation[4] is frequently used in the academic world to convey the idea that authority is granted to direct reports to perform their work. In organizational settings, the term is commonly used to address problems with managers' workload and schedules. In the latter case, it is seen as an antidote to micromanagement and a major step towards improving a manager's performance.

However, the term does not seem to impart any helpful insight when used to indicate that authority is granted to direct reports to perform their work, even if the authority granted to a direct report is associated with the creation of a new management level. The redistribution of non-managerial work performed by a manager, regardless of whether it is passed on to a manager or a non-manager, and the creation of a new managerial level should not be considered delegation. Instead, such measures should be seen as part of the normal process of departmentalization.

The term delegation makes more sense and has better application if reserved to mean the handing over of parts of or entire management functions to direct reports without creating a new management level and without divesting a manager of the primary responsibility over what is being delegated. As discussed earlier, parts of some functions, like the obtention of less costly resources that are the duty of the Provisioning function, are very suited to delegation.

Delegation can be used at any management level, and functions can be delegated to both managers and non-managers. Furthermore, delegation can be employed on an ad-hoc basis, which might avoid triggering changes to a direct report's job description, this way preserving the arrangement of the work area.

The trade-off is that while the span of management increases with delegation, the measure tends to make the integration of the management functions rather more complex.

5.4 Decentralization

To decentralize is to let go of part of a manager's area of responsibility—to reduce the span of both direct and indirect management.

Decentralization[5] entails change in the organizational structure, affecting activities, functional areas, business units, and so on. This is accomplished by spinning off part of the work done by direct reports under a particular manager. For example, a Sales Department could be formed as the result of its separation from a Marketing Department. It does not matter if the new area has the same, higher, or lower hierarchical level as the one from where it originated. The essential requirement is that the two areas should not have a managerial connection where a relationship between a manager and a direct or indirect report exists. This means that completely separate management is necessary for the new area being created.

The creation of new hierarchical levels under a manager's span of management should not be confused with decentralization. Using the example above, even though the Sales Department is no longer under the responsibility of the Marketing manager, it is still supposedly under the responsibility of the same Commercial Manager (Vice President), and certainly still indirectly under the same responsibility of a higher manager like a CEO. Hence, at a given time in an organization, decentralization might affect some managers and not others.

Decentralization can be pursued for strategic or political purposes. However, perhaps the most frequent occasion to consider it is when the span of direct plus indirect management becomes too much for a manager to handle. In other words, the most basic concern driving decentralization should be the creation of work areas that are more manageable and productive.

Some Factors that Can Affect the Span of Direct Management

- Number of areas
- Number of direct reports
- Level of direct reports autonomy
- Level of direct reports involvement
- Level of delegation
- Level of formality
- Type of direct report
  - Manager
  - Non-manager
- Nature of direct report
  - Individual – single or arranged in work group(s)
  - Team – single or arranged in work group(s)

Table 5

6

Manager's Personal Qualities

It might well be that there is no particular personality type that is required to be a manager. This issue is even more complex because personality types must be combined with other factors, like personal qualities and scientific and technological knowledge, for a manager to be able to fulfill his or her role adequately. However, like management functions that remain the same at all levels, some basic qualities[1] should be present in all managers.

That said, different management levels might benefit from certain personality traits and complementary qualities. As a result, different lists can be made of complementary qualities relevant for people to be successful managers at different management levels. Other lists could result from considerations like the type of organization, type of industry, or cultural context.

Regardless, everybody must be conscious that, above all, any list of qualities is an expression of an individual understanding of human reality. Not only is each person drawn to focus on different qualities, but also managers, like everyone else, manifest qualities that are the result of their own understanding of this reality. This understanding shapes each individual's thoughts, decisions, and actions.

The list of basic personal qualities that is being presented here, which in practice has well proven its value, is aligned with the concept of human beings as social beings, and consequently with that of the organization as an instrument for individual and collective prosperity.

6.1 Self-Mastery

The topic of self-mastery[2] is considered pertinent enough to be discussed in other management materials. Here, however, it is being presented from a new and deeper perspective, a perspective that places managers in harmony with the collective.

It is true that self-mastery has to do with the capacity for self-control and self-discipline. Yet, the deepening in understanding comes from the recognition that one attains self-mastery not by focusing on oneself, but instead by forgetting oneself*.

> The 'Master Key' to self-mastery is self-forgetting.[3]
>
> 'Abdu'l-Bahá

Paying persistent attention to oneself can lead to being proud of oneself or feeling sorry for oneself. The former leads to aggrandizing, the later to the diminishing of oneself. Both feed the ego. Ego leads to a fruitless and insatiable search for self-satisfaction. In other words, centering one's attention on oneself feeds our animalistic nature, which results in a loss of self-control.

> The other self is the ego, the dark, animalistic heritage each one of us has, the lower nature that can develop into a monster of selfishness, brutality, lust and so on.[4]
>
> From a letter written on behalf of Shoghi Effendi

---

* This proposition does not mean that one does not have to examine oneself regularly. "Focusing on" oneself is different from "examining" oneself.

Consequently, we might say that ego, or "insistent self", is a spiritual disease that thrives on attention.

In the context of organizations, ego avails itself of abuse of authority (in the case of managers), manipulation, politics, competition, and so on, in the attempt to fulfill personal desires at any cost. With such behavior comes disrespect, dishonesty, and conflict, not to mention the negative material impact on the lives of many.

On the other hand, by forgetting oneself, one allows positive qualities, like truthfulness, humility, patience, courtesy, compassion, trustworthiness, and justice, to flourish, all of which lead to cooperation, teamwork, service, and happiness.

In one sense, self-forgetting is not an easy thing to do. On the other hand, it can easily be done if one succeeds in becoming altruistic, by replacing, or occupying, one's thoughts with something else other than with oneself.

> *Do not busy yourselves in your own concerns; let your thoughts be fixed upon that which will rehabilitate the fortunes of mankind and sanctify the hearts and souls of men.*[5]
>
> Bahá'u'lláh

Certainly, altruism is essential to the development of every human being. However, in the case of managers who have to position themselves as facilitators of collective production and be involved with other people's work, altruism is also a professional necessity. Definitely, the need for managers to manifest such a quality cannot be considered to have the same impact on the functioning of the organization as that of non-managers.

Managers should not allow their status to take over. They need to forget their personal interests and master themselves in order to be able to behave appropriately in their role as facilitators. If a facilitator takes center stage, the de facto players are constrained in the full execution of their work, causing a reversal of purposes. It would be like a soccer coach stepping in and asking for the ball in the middle of a game.

6.2 People Skills

The concept of people skills is commonly associated with the type of person who is extroverted and engaging, and typically the center of attention. To some extent, organizations expect managers, especially the good ones, to fit this stereotype. However, experience has shown that managers can have very different personalities, even completely opposite to the type described above, and still be very successful.

Complementing such expectations is the notion that managers should master subjects like personality traits, perceptions, assumptions, influence, feedback, motivational factors, group dynamics, power, and politics. It is as if managers should also be psychologists in order to better analyze and interact with their direct reports and other stakeholders.

However, a sure and simplified way for managers to deal with the issue of human interaction in an extremely fitting manner is by using the *Golden Rule*[6].

The Golden Rule, for those who do not remember it, is the rule that states that one should treat others the same way as, or better than, one would like to be treated. It is not without reason that this universal rule has been emphasized repeatedly throughout human history by all religions. The pity is that not only does it seem that this rule for the most part has fallen onto deaf ears, but it also seems that many believe it does not apply to work settings. However, this is definitely not the case.

The reality is that every human deserves to be treated with respect, courtesy, kindness, and justice, regardless of context, so managers must treat their direct reports and everybody else accordingly, as well as expect equal behavior from any stakeholder over whom he has authority.

The burden of the success of relationships lies mostly with managers because of their function of authority. Formal authority causes others to relate to them with a certain deference. Above all, direct reports are in a position where they are formally compelled to exercise self-restraint. The same does not happen with managers, which can unfortunately lead some to relax in their responsibility of exercising self-control. Consequently, managers are often the ones setting the tone for interactions, while direct reports, on the receiving end, generally try to keep a positive or neutral attitude at the start. Usually the receivers, especially in a context of difference in degrees, tend to react in accordance with the agent who initiates the interaction. For instance, if one shows love, the other tends to respond with love and cooperation. On the other hand, if one shows hate, the other tends to reciprocate with hate and opposition.

It should be noted that at the core of the Golden Rule is the principle of justice.

> *...if thine eyes be turned towards justice, choose thou for thy neighbour that which thou choosest for thyself.*[7]
>
> Bahá'u'lláh

How can one harmonize multiple needs and capacities, handle conflict, build trust, properly communicate with others, and value diversity without exercising justice? When there is justice, there is no room for politics, hidden agendas, blame games, power, influence, coercion, and so on. With justice, there is no space for discrimination between direct reports, peers, superiors, clients, providers, oneself and others.

Fair managers, regardless of their personalities, have no problem at all interacting with their direct reports. They may be extroverted or introverted, funny or serious. As long as they are able to treat others using the Golden Rule, the element of their work that deals with human interaction can be satisfactorily addressed. In fact, people's capacity to work together with cooperation increases with the exercise of justice.

Though he or she might not become everyone's pal, everyone is surely more than pleased to work with a fair manager.

6.2.1 Justice

Because an organization is a system and a system is a group of interdependent parts where the parts contribute to and benefit from the whole, the power of justice is essential to harmonize the diverse individual needs and the group's needs. In addition, because organizations are systems within other systems, interdependence is extended and justice must be applied to harmonize the needs of others outside each organization. Thus, justice has the essential function of balancing society.

> *The purpose of justice is the appearance of unity among men.*[8]
>
> Bahá'u'lláh

Still, in management not nearly enough attention has been paid to the question of justice. To say the least, the way the matter has been treated falls short of its importance to humans, organizations, and society.

Although academic schools have paid somewhat more attention to this question than the practical world has, they too, for the most part, have fallen short in leading any significant discussion of the role of justice and its implications.

In the academic world, the topic has been more the concern of researchers than a relevant feature in management courses. In general, management courses address the subject of justice briefly, if at all, by imparting the following perspectives[9]:

1. *Distributive Justice* – The dispensing of rewards and penalties according to the hierarchical position of each individual in the organization. It relates to the assignment of work and the provisions to carry it out, as well as to the produced deliverables.

2. *Procedural Justice* – The extent of transparency in the process of distributing rewards and penalties throughout the organization.

3. *Interactional Justice* – The actual level of distributive and procedural justice received and/or understood by each individual.

As a result, academic studies on the subject have not been easily transferable to the practical world. For the most part, managers have been left with considerable room to implement justice in accordance with their individual consciousness, based on their particular vision of human beings and of society. This freedom is only guided or constrained to the extent that society's laws penetrate their organizations.

Because in management, justice is manifested in every decision and displayed in each function, as managers endeavor to facilitate collective work, the unifying force of justice must be consistently employed. Thus, in daily management, justice must be further considered, discussed, and practiced from the standpoint of its purpose and implications, both at the individual and collective levels.

- "At the individual level, justice is that faculty of the human soul that enables each person to distinguish truth from falsehood".

- "At the group level …justice is the practical expression of awareness that, in the achievement of human progress, the interests of the individual and those of society* are inextricably linked".

Justice is the one power that can translate the dawning consciousness of humanity's oneness into a collective will through which the necessary structures of global community life can be confidently erected. An age that sees the people of the world increasingly gaining access to information of every kind and to a diversity of ideas will find justice asserting itself as the ruling principle of successful social organization. With ever-greater frequency, proposals aiming at the development of the planet will have to submit to the candid light of the standards it requires.

At the individual level, justice is that faculty of the human soul that enables each person to distinguish truth from falsehood. In the sight of God, Bahá'u'lláh avers, justice is "the best beloved of all things" since it permits each individual to see with his own eyes rather than the eyes of others, to know through his own knowledge rather than the knowledge of his neighbor or his group. It calls for fair-mindedness in one's judgments, for equity in one's treatment of others, and is thus a constant if demanding companion in the daily occasions of life.

At the group level, a concern for justice is the indispensable compass in collective decision making, because it is the only means by which unity of thought and action can be achieved. Far from encouraging the punitive spirit that has often masqueraded under its name in past ages, justice is the practical expression of awareness that, in the achievement of human progress, the interests of the individual and those of society are inextricably linked. To the extent that justice becomes a guiding concern of human interaction, a consultative climate is encouraged that permits options to be examined dispassionately and appropriate courses of action selected. In such a climate the perennial tendencies toward manipulation and partisanship are far less likely to deflect the decision-making process.[10]

Bahá'í International Community

---

* An organization can be analogous to society.

6.2.2 Consultation

Consultation is a group decision-making method specific for channeling justice. Through it, the manifestation of justice at both individual and group levels reaches new heights.

> Central to the task of reconceptualizing the system of human relationships is the process that Bahá'u'lláh refers to as consultation "In all things it is necessary to consult," is His advice "The maturity of the gift of understanding is made manifest through consultation.
>
> The standard of truth seeking this process demands is far beyond the patterns of negotiation and compromise that tend to characterize the present-day discussion of human affairs. It cannot be achieved — indeed, its attainment is severely handicapped — by the culture of protest that is another widely prevailing feature of contemporary society. Debate, propaganda, the adversarial method, the entire apparatus of partisanship that have long been such familiar features of collective action are all fundamentally harmful to its purpose: that is, arriving at a consensus about the truth of a given situation and the wisest choice of action among the options open at any given moment.
>
> What Bahá'u'lláh is calling for is a consultative process in which the individual participants strive to transcend their respective points of view, in order to function as members of a body with its own interests and goals. In such an atmosphere, characterized by both candor and courtesy, ideas belong not to the individual to whom they occur during the discussion but to the group as a whole, to take up, discard, or revise as seems to best serve the goal pursued. Consultation succeeds to the extent that all participants support the decisions arrived at, regardless of the individual opinions with which they entered the discussion. Under such circumstances, an earlier decision can be readily reconsidered if experience exposes any shortcomings.
>
> Viewed in such a light, consultation is the operating expression of justice in human affairs. So vital is it to the success of collective endeavor that it must constitute a basic feature of a viable strategy of social and economic development. Indeed, the participation of the people on whose commitment and efforts the success of such a strategy depends becomes effective only as consultation is made the organizing principle of every project. "No man can attain his true station," is Bahá'u'lláh's

counsel, "except through his justice. No power can exist except through unity. No welfare and no well-being can be attained except through consultation.[11]

Bahá'í International Community

A note should be made regarding conflict, which some people believe, like competition, to be good. They reason that conflict is the best, and perhaps only, medicine for a problem like *Groupthink**. The rationale is that conflict takes people from their comfort zone and forces them to achieve a level of performance that they would otherwise never achieve. Aside from the fact that nearly every person feels deeply uncomfortable, if not sick to their stomach in situations of conflict and, therefore, almost no one seems to go around consciously creating strife or quarrels in organizations, conflict in effect creates disunity and is destructive. Even if conflict, regardless of its intensity, is capable of creating any benefit at all, along the way it subtracts more than what it can possibly add. At the end of every conflictive process, the final balance is always negative. That said, there is a truth enshrined in the test of ideas.

The shining spark of truth cometh forth only after the clash of differing opinions.[13]

'Abdu'l-Bahá

The main difference that characterizes this "clash of differing opinions" in consultation compared to the clashing that happens in regular conflict is that the former takes place in the context of unity, while the latter is the outcome of opposing parties. In other words, conflict only happens because contrary sides struggle with each other, but when there are no sides, when there is only one entity, conflict cannot possibly exist.

This is most easily seen in the example of an individual who is exploring and comparing different alternatives. Unless he is mentally ill, he does not get offended, upset or fight with him or herself.

In other words, if consultation is carried out correctly, if individual ego is not involved, conflict cannot occur because there are no parts to oppose each other—"the ideas belong to the group". The group functions like a single individual exploring different options.

---

* Expression created to explain group consensus around a bad proposition with the intention of avoiding disunity. For more about Groupthink, see endnote number 12.

Consequently, consultation is a group decision-making method that can make management easy.

- It is perfect for shared management
- It can contribute to all management functions
- It can perfect managers' people skills
- It goes beyond the empowerment and involvement of direct reports
- It brings about the results of trust and collaboration, and a healthy work environment becomes the norm
- It generates synergy that increases creativity, accuracy of decisions and success in implementation
- It transforms organizations into high performance systems

6.3 Self-Organization

In nature, everything that is thriving is organized. On the other hand, disorganization, and at a more advanced stage chaos, is a sign that something is not well and might be on a path to failing or perishing.

Even our inner and social realities are subject to organization. Consider, for example, our thoughts. What can we produce if our thoughts are not organized? We need organized words to formulate thoughts, and organized thoughts to live well. Even single images that we can generate in our minds are composite organized realities. Thus, the more organized the association of elements and ideas, the more advanced and complex a reality can be.

People might be inclined to think that order stifles creativity, but this is not the case. Creativity is better put to use by reflecting deeply on issues, by expanding one's knowledge of reality.

The source of crafts, sciences and arts is the power of reflection.[14]

Bahá'u'lláh

The issue of organization should be of paramount importance for managers as individuals, as it is to institutional order. The managerial position demands the employment of a combination of diversified measures to deal with multiple elements in a state of dynamic interplay. If a manager is not reasonably well-organized, he or she most likely will not be able to handle the complexity of his or her work, and will get "lost" in the midst of an organic system.

Managers should be organized both internally and externally. Their thoughts, schedules, desks, files, and so forth, must all be organized. If he or she cannot organize those things that are within his or her personal sphere, how can such a person be expected to organize work groups, ranging from small units to large corporations? Consequently, self-organization should be one of a manager's most discernible qualities.

A manager's lack of time might be linked to different factors, but it is ultimately proportional to his or her level of organization. To assist managers in dealing with this issue, subjects like time-management, self-management, personal productivity, and work-life balance have been developed. Although in many cases these subjects go beyond addressing the matter of organizing, the issue of order is (or should be) at their core. That being the case, a simple and yet powerful tool that can greatly assist managers with personal organization is scheduling. Of course, once a schedule is created, one has to stick to it. Being disciplined is fundamental. Additionally, well-designed structures can be very helpful. Many see organizational structure as a driver of behavior[15]. This understanding might not be one hundred percent true, but by establishing good lines of relations, structure makes managers' lives easier.

Ideally, the quality of self-organization should be acquired during one's upbringing, but if such an opportunity has been missed, it is still possible for someone with determination to develop it later in life.

In any case, with or without the assistance of managerial tools and methodologies, self-organization, like any other quality, has to become part of one's philosophy of life. If embraced, it should be manifested at work and in every other sphere of life. This is the only way for a manager to stay organized.

6.4 Thinker

As mentioned before in the topic Intrapersonal Work Domain, a significant portion of managerial work is intellectual in nature—that is, it is abstract, rather than being readily perceptible by the senses. Hence, managers cannot simply rely on quick thinking and feelings to properly address intellectual work, especially in intricate and fluid environments.

To dedicate the appropriate level of consideration required by many aspects of their work, managers have to allot time for reflection. They can benefit even more if they take it a step further and also embrace the practice of meditation*.

Reflection and meditation are sometimes used synonymously, but here a distinction in degree is being made between the two. Reflection is a more easily reachable frame of mind where one carefully considers a subject, while meditation goes further and takes one to a state of profound concentration, where the senses are not allowed to be a distraction.

To better understand the operation of reflection and meditation, one has to consider a human reality that goes beyond our physical existence[16].

For example, some people believe that we as humans do not use one hundred percent of our brain, and, therefore, we potentially have much more capacity than what we actually use. While it is true that most of us do not tap into our full capacity, the reason for this underuse is not related to the brain. It is due to one not posing enough, if at all, questions to one's spirit through the faculty of meditation.

> *The spirit of man is itself informed and strengthened during meditation; through it affairs of which man knew nothing are unfolded before his view.*
>
> *…This faculty brings forth from the invisible plane the sciences and arts. Through the meditative faculty inventions are made possible, colossal undertakings are carried out; through it governments can run smoothly.[17]*
>
> 'Abdu'l-Bahá

This does not mean that managers must stop to reflect or meditate every time that they deal with abstract work. It does mean that managers should occasionally take the time to reflect or meditate to try to deepen their understanding of particular realities that are continuously changing.

For instance, when managers encounter a new concept or are analyzing the operations, developing a strategy, or searching for a solution to a problem, they might take some time to reflect or meditate upon such issues. It

---

* There are different approaches to meditation. At the opposite ends of the spectrum, one approach tries to clear one's mind, while the other engages in a deep conversation with one's spirit.

would be helpful for managers to do this before entering into consultation with others. This means that consultation and reflection or meditation should not be used to the exclusion of each other. Instead, they should complement each other.

Neither reflection nor meditation necessitates sophisticated process or technique, but they do improve with practice. Simply put, reflection and meditation can be carried out by focusing on specific topics, of posing questions to one's spirit and receiving the answers from it. Both functions benefit from silence and isolation from possible disturbances, given that, as mentioned above, to reach a state of meditation one needs to completely withdraw one's attention from the objective world.

As such, time for reflection and/or meditation should be included in a manager's schedule or arranged for another convenient time of the day, even if at bedtime. Managers do not have to become philosophers, but they must be willing to develop the habit of reflecting, and possibly of meditating. It might also be that reflection and meditation have the potential for greatly helping managers to train their minds and to lessen their *Knowing-Doing Gap**.

---

* Gap between what one knows and what one puts into practice. For more about the Knowing-Doing Gap, see endnote number 18.

7

Managers' Approaches

If, on the one hand, no person can have a truly holistic view, on the other hand, attempts to concentrate exclusively on a single aspect of a reality in order to adequately comprehend it are not feasible either. To be able to reach deep levels of understanding, it is imperative to combine narrow and broad, departmentalized and holistic approaches. Hence, serious specialization can only come about by increasing the understanding of a particular entity or phenomenon to encompass the system(s) of which it is a part.

Understanding, then, can be pursued by having individuals focusing on single elements of reality, while building a holistic view through collectivity. This means that it would be ideal for an individual to try to learn as much as possible about a single subject, and at the same time a little bit about everything else, to be better able to integrate his or her knowledge with that of the others.

In management, an individual's propensity to focus on single issues might be manifested through a manager's dedication towards a particular element of the organization, which can sometimes lead to an unconscious neglect of others. As a result, and as a natural extension of this effort, the manager ends up making disproportionate use of a specific management function while overlooking others.

Some of the reasons that might contribute to an over emphasis of one specific function could be:

- The belief that a specific element of the organization has the potential of being the key contributor to its overall success
- Personal affinity with a specific organizational element
- More experience with a certain management function
- Influence from the environment – area of specialization, organizational culture, type of organization, industry, and so forth
- The impulse to embrace the fad of the time

By gaining awareness of and evaluating their preferences for certain functions, managers might be able to compensate for any unhealthy imbalance through individual effort and/or group participation.

Hence, this chapter concisely presents a classification using four categories of managers' approaches towards their work, plus a fifth one that is the combination of the other four.

7.1 Strategy-Oriented

The strategy-oriented approach is embraced by managers who believe that strategy, and by extension visions and objectives, is at the heart of an organization's success.

These managers, of course, tend to be good strategic thinkers, very concerned with external as well as internal factors and holistic formulations. Consequently, a lot of time is dedicated to environmental analysis and strategic formulation.

Managers who center their attention on strategy might be inclined to favor marketing above other areas of specialization in the organization. They are more open to listening and reacting to external demands.

For strategy-oriented managers, (strategic) Planning is of course the main management function, seconded by Monitoring to ensure adherence to plan.

7.2 Operation-Oriented

Managers who see the production of deliverables as the obvious way to fulfill the organization's mission are inclined to concentrate their efforts on operation.

The main field of action for these operation-oriented managers is the formal sphere of the organization. They might strive for operational excellence by pressing for efficient structures and processes with the assistance of management programs, like Total Quality Management, Six Sigma, Quality Circles, and Just-in-time.

Therefore, the Coordinating function is of greatest importance to managers driven by production concerns, with Organizing and Monitoring coming closely in second and Provisioning in a slightly more distant third place.

7.3 People-Oriented

Managers who are people-oriented usually see humans as the cause and the end beneficiary of every organizational endeavor. As a result, some of these managers are inclined to consider the organizations' materialistic objectives as secondary to human well-being.

In this case, special attention is paid to the informal aspect of the organization, such as culture, organization fit, and to staff development and happiness.

Many managers in this category like to avail themselves of leadership and coaching to involve, motivate, and empower direct reports, and to develop team spirit. Rewards are substantially extended to non-financial benefits and human conflict is avoided as much as possible. One of the main aims of people-oriented managers is the creation of a work environment where individual loyalty to the organization is experienced as a source of joy, and honest concern to customers' and other stakeholders' satisfaction becomes the norm.

These managers tend to dedicate a considerable amount of time to human interaction. Where for some other managers a 10-minute meeting would suffice, human interaction with people-oriented managers can easily take up to an hour or more, as they tend to branch out into conversations on multiple topics.

For people-oriented managers, Customer Intimacy might end up being the organizational competence to master, with Leadership, Supporting and Cultural Modeling as the most emphasized management functions.

7.4 Knowledge-Oriented

What would humans be without knowledge? Would organizations exist without it? If knowledge seems to be at the foundation of organizations, it must then be at the core of their success.

Managers who are knowledge-oriented are very much motivated by the search for the next big idea, for the next invention that will transform the world. Their focus is on the development of cutting-edge technology, which requires the creation of the right conditions to allow and stimulate creativity and foster innovation.

In such a context, learning becomes a major concern, but not necessarily learning gained through the acquisition of new information and new skills. What is sought is the creation of a learning mode where new knowledge can be discovered—a learning mode that could be explained as a spirit, a posture of constant investigation, or a revision of an ever changing reality, which in turn deepens understanding of old and new compositions, connections, dynamics, and so forth.

Organizations managed with emphasis on this approach, generally build their core competence around research and development of new deliverables.

To fulfill this purpose, the function of Cultural Modeling, complemented by Provisioning (especially of personnel and technology) is considered a top priority.

7.5 Balance-Oriented

The truth is that organizations only come to exist because a great number of elements, like people, knowledge, equipment, and raw materials, come into collective play by way of specific arrangements and processes. It is not possible to have an organization without people or knowledge or operation; nor is it possible to have much success without strategy. For this reason, management needs to move beyond emphasis on a specific approach and consider a holistic, balanced modus operandi.

While focus on a particular element of the organization has its value and moment of need, alone it is not enough. Single approaches or functions cannot be turned into one-size-fits-all solutions. A manager's approach has to expand to include all functions and be concerned with all main elements of an organization.

By having an equal regard for all functions, not only are managers considering a holistic approach, but they also end up exercising moderation. Of course, this does not mean that all functions have to, or can be, executed simultaneously. In fact, due to a human being's incapacity to do more than one thing at any given time[1], one management function should be prioritized over the others in accordance with the needs of the moment.

In overcoming emphasis on specific elements of the organization, managers can hardly depend exclusively on awareness and self-discipline. The best route is through shared management, especially, if possible, by involving people of different backgrounds, personalities, ages, genders, and so forth.

8

Shared Management

Although this book does not approach management from the perspective of addressing the challenges faced by the profession, it does touch on some of these difficulties and some concepts crucial to overcoming them.

Paramount among these concepts is the notion of shared management that includes as many people as possible in the decision-making. Not only is shared management through group decision-making extremely useful in improving the execution of management functions, but it is also essential to allow for a more consistent application of justice.

The socialization of management through the inclusion of more people in the decision-making can and should happen in different ways, none of them to the exclusion of others. For example, managers should consult with their direct reports, peers, clients, and other stakeholders as regularly as it is feasible. Indeed, a culture should be created where everyone is constantly trying to involve others in decision-making. However, as addressed before, it is not practical for everybody to be directly involved in every single decision. In particular, universal participation becomes trickier at organization levels different from one's own. This means that moderation and wisdom must be part of every decision-making process. In sizeable organizations, large-scale collective decision-making is mostly practical by means of *cascading** and/or by general assembly meetings.

It should be noted that the purpose of both general assembly meetings and cascading does not necessarily have to be to arrive at a decision. These events can be used primarily for the decision-making phases related to the exploration of subjects in question, which means that some people participate in only certain phases of the process.

It might be possible to say that any fair process of decision making rests on the identification of issues, ascertainment of facts, identification of principles involved, and the selection of a course of action[1]. Consequently, being true to this concept, it is possible to conclude that contributions to all but one of the decision-making phases—that is, to the selection of a course of action—can still be classified as active participation. Of course, for this arrangement to be valid, it is necessary for the final phase to be faithful to the process as a whole. In other words, those coming to a decision must take into consideration the input that has been generated before them. However, considering input does not mean that the ideas raised before must be included in the final decision. It means that they should be dispassionately deliberated on during the final stage.

In practical terms then, cascading involves representatives of different work areas functioning as delegates (often the area's manager) to meet and make decisions on behalf of members of their groups. The representatives bring the input from their fellow group members to the next phase of the process, a duty that requires an altruistic attitude and a concern for collectivity.

That being the case, there are two complementary ways organizations might implement shared management:

1. *Occasional shared management* – This can occur through managers' formal and/or informal consultations with their direct reports, work groups, general assemblies, and so forth.

---

* Happening in stages. Representatives of one organizational level usually carry the process to another level.

2. *Uninterrupted shared management carried out by teams* – This means inserting teams into managerial positions.

In this case, the composition of such teams can be as follows:

- Hierarchically equal members, like:
    o Board of directors
    o X numbers of co-CEOs

- Hierarchically different members (cheapest composition), like President with Vice-Presidents—A better representation would be Executive Secretary (President) of a committee with Executive Secretaries (Vice-Presidents) of sub-committees. That is, teams composed of managers and their direct reports, with the direct reports being managers or non-managers.

Regardless of composition, the major challenge and solution for uninterrupted shared management is to be found in the appropriate assignment of roles and responsibilities, of both individuals and the team as a whole. If this is not done well, the arrangement runs a high risk of turning into an army of generals without soldiers.

The most pertinent aspect of this assignment of roles and responsibilities is the correct distribution of management functions between the team and the single team member who should serve as Executive Secretary.

The team can assume management functions like Planning, Cultural Modeling, and Monitoring of mid and long-term performance, plus key Provisioning, Organizing, and problem solving. The Executive Secretary can be in charge of duties such as Coordinating, Supporting, Liaising, Monitoring of short-term performance, and some less relevant problem solving, Provisioning, and Organizing.

With this type of arrangement, the team would meet on a less regular basis, something like once a week or twice a month, to deal with team members' areas and consult on issues of broad interest. Outside team meetings, the Executive Secretary functions as an individual manager and is responsible for overseeing the implementation of the decisions made by the team. In such circumstances, the other team members operate as the Secretary's direct reports.

Without a doubt, one of shared management's main benefits is its capacity to allow for a deeper understanding, making it simpler to diagnose complex problems and design better solutions. Still, perhaps the most relevant factor is that through shared management it is exceedingly more feasible to exercise justice. What work group or team would not want to be less vulnerable to personal agendas and mood swings of individual managers? That is to say, what work group or team would not want to lessen the influence and concentration of authority on single individuals?

PART III

Supplement

Relation of Part III to Management Functions

Most management publications are not categorized or written in a way that makes it clear how they relate to management functions. This omission seems to make it more difficult for many people to understand the discipline of management. Hence, the chapters in Part III of this book are presented in part as an attempt to assist managers to better understand many of the ideas that comprise their profession.

Some categories that can help clarify how this large portion of the body of ideas relates to management functions are:

Category	Relation to Management Functions
Management Tools	Instruments that contribute to the execution of management functions
Management Programs	Customized methods for carrying out part, one, or several management functions
Managers' Functional Areas of Expertise	Specialized areas of collective production, often with a sufficient number of personnel and complexity of processes to accommodate individuals dedicated exclusively to managerial work

Table P-III

9

Management Tools

Management tools[1] are instruments that contribute to, but are not components of, management functions, so it is possible for managers to carry out their duties without them. However, in many instances, doing so might not be very prudent, as the correct utilization of some tools can prove to be the difference between success and failure.

Consider, for example, the use of cash flow projections. A manager might be able to help an organization keep up with the payment of bills for a while, but without the assistance of such a tool, it is just a matter of time until the organization runs into trouble. Another example could be that of a manager who has the capacity to organize some work areas without the assistance of tools like an organizational chart, flowchart, or job description. However, as the complexity of the organization increases, if tools like these are not used, chances are that inefficiency will prevail.

It is interesting to note that most people think of management tools as being very complex and hard to learn, but though some are more sophisticated, most are actually quite simple.

In general, the challenge resides not in the tools themselves, but in how to get them to add significant value to what managers are actually supposed to do. This means that their enhanced utilization has to be grounded on a solid understanding of what management work is about. Managers should be able to benefit even more from the utilization of management tools if they observe clear links between the tools and the execution of particular management functions. Additionally, they should expand their focus in order to broaden the utilization of tools beyond the formal sphere of the organization.

One example of a fantastic, yet simple, management tool is the personal schedule. Although a personal schedule is not a complex tool, its usefulness is directly proportional to a manager's capacity to properly represent his work in it, and of course, adhere to it.

Another example of an often-misunderstood tool, though it can be reasonably more complex, is the audit. Unfortunately, audits, especially financial ones, are almost exclusively associated with the intent of uncovering mismanagement, embezzlement, and so forth. The reality is that there are many different reasons why audits should be performed. Among those reasons are their usefulness in helping improve operations, communications, and trust.

Since the objective here is not to provide a thorough list of management tools, just a few of them are being presented in a somewhat detailed manner, while others are being listed as possible references.

9.1 Personal Schedules

A personal schedule is a vital management tool. It is so important that if it were possible to assign the label of "The First Tool" to a management tool, the personal schedule probably would receive such a distinction. Through it, managers organize their work and establish the foundation of their performance.

Without a good schedule, managers might not find enough time to deal with all their responsibilities. In fact, they might possibly be on the path to chaos.

The initial guiding instrument managers should use in the development of their schedule is the organizational chart, followed by their job description.

The sample schedule below was designed for the CEO of a privately held mid-sized company.

Morning period

First Hour

    A. Keep abreast of issues directly and indirectly related to the business – read news (at least summaries), technical articles, government policies and regulations

    B. Take care of correspondence and/or instruct secretary on how to handle it

    C. Assign and/or review secretary's tasks

    D. Process small tasks – authorize large payments, sign contracts

Second Hour

    E. Reflect or meditate on issues – analyze reports, performance indicators (of direct reports, work groups, organization)

    F. Prepare for meetings, presentations

Third & Fourth Hours

    G. Meet with direct reports

Afternoon period

    H. Work on special projects, major problem-solving, new planning cycle

    I. Attend extra non-recurring meetings; give presentations

    J. Receive key external agents: clients, providers, suppliers

    K. Attend external commitments: visit external sites, key suppliers, other key stakeholders, events

    L. Meet with the rest of staff, make general announcements, celebrate birthdays and milestones

Personal Schedule

Time	Mon	Tue	Wed	Thu	Fri
8-9 a.m.	Duties A,B,C, & D	Duties A,B,C, & D	Duties A,B,C, & D	Duties A,B,C, & D	Duties A,B,C, & D
9-10 a.m.	Duties E & F	Duties E & F	Duties E & F	Duties E & F	Duties E & F
10-12 a.m.	Duty G (VP of Finance)	Duty G (VP of Operations)	Duty G (VP of Marketing)	Duty G (VP of Adm.)	Duty G* (All VPs / Consultative Council)
1-5 p.m.	Duties I – K	Duties I – K	Duties I – K	Duties I – K	Duties I – K or L**

Table 9.1

Notes:

* Bi-weekly

** Monthly (Aside from a plenary meeting for general announcements and celebrations, when meeting with the rest of the staff, the CEO can, for instance, allocate 20-30 minutes to meet with individual departments.)

The above schedule clearly takes into account the organizational structure, that is, the boundaries of the direct span of management, and the job description. It allots time for the execution of all management functions, demonstrating a balanced management approach. At the same time, it also incorporates other major management concepts like shared management and consideration for different working domains, even dedicating time to the practice of meditation.

9.2 Meetings

Meetings[2] are one of the most widely used tools in management because they serve as a major venue for the execution of management functions. However, it is not as simple as it might seem for managers to make use of them. To some extent, this difficulty exists because the quality of a meeting is directly related to the manager's capacity to perform his or her diverse functions. In other words, in a single meeting, several management functions might be required, and perhaps executed, but a lack of awareness of this can become a major obstacle for achieving satisfactory results.

Additionally, the level of subjectivism and dynamism occurring in groups with more than two persons can greatly increase the challenge of managing meetings. Addressing this challenge might require managers to develop, for example, the skill of handling the interplay of large amounts of data, feelings, and thoughts conveyed primarily through words and body language*. This skill is important because without it managers can have a hard time assisting with the testing of ideas and formulation of group decisions. Uncertain or complex matters can greatly affect such interplay between meeting participants. Depending on the maturity level of the participants, managers might also have to be prepared to deal with issues such as competing interests, hidden agendas, and the formation of sub-groups.

As discussed before, consultation is a panacea for human interaction and a must for group meetings. If correctly practiced, consultation eliminates negative human dynamics, immensely facilitating managers' work. That said, some elements that should be considered concerning the more technical aspect of consultation and meetings, especially for recurring formal meetings, are:

- Agenda
- Decision-making process
- Group's norms, plus mission and visions in the case of teams
- Meeting structure
- Meetings – complementary phases of preparation and implementation
- Minutes
- Roles and responsibilities, as imparted by the positions of chairperson (may be rotating) and recording secretary, and in the case of teams, the extra positions of vice-chairperson, executive secretary, correspondence secretary, and so on

1. Meeting preparation

   Meeting preparation starts with special consideration about who should participate in it. It might sound obvious, but key people are not always invited, while sometimes people who do not have much to contribute show up, at everyone's expense. As mentioned before, diversity is another important matter to be taken into account.

---

* Body language, either in support of or in objection to someone's contribution, is generally counterproductive to group decision-making.

The preparation process continues with the creation of an agenda. Although agendas can, and often are, adjusted at the beginning of meetings, their creation has to start well in advance. In fact, for recurring meetings, creation of the agenda could even start at the end of a previous meeting. In other words, the outlining of the agenda for the next meeting can be a regular last item on the current agenda.

The agenda should be drafted by more than one person, in general the executive secretary and the chair, but all participants can and should contribute to it. Once finalized, all meeting participants should receive a copy in a timely manner prior to the next meeting.

If a topic is not ready for consultation, for example, if there is insufficient information, it should not be added to the agenda. All facts need to be verified as much as possible before being presented at meetings. Perceptions, vague recollection of events and imprecise data can easily lead to endless discussions, possible conflicts, and bad decisions. This being the case, before each meeting, all meeting participants should receive, aside from the agenda, a reasonable amount of accurate information related to each topic, if applicable. This enables those not primarily responsible for specific topics to prepare for the meetings, and even to perform their own additional research if necessary.

It can be helpful to cover related topics in sequence. In addition, the necessary time to deal with each individual topic should be estimated in advance. If it turns out that a topic needs more time, it might be addressed again later, so as not to compromise the rest of the agenda. In any case, what should be prevented as much as possible is making decisions under the pressure of time.

If planning to use consultation, one thing that also should be avoided, contrary to what is sometimes suggested, is the determination of "desired outcomes". Visions and objectives should guide the work, but nothing should try to force meeting results. Consultation calls for an open-minded attitude that accepts that the results are not known beforehand. Consequently, all participants must be detached from their own initial ideas and opinions, and open to any outcome.

In addition to the list of items for consultation, agendas should also include things like a heading (similar to minutes, indicating the group's name, participants, location, date, time, and numbering) and a responsibility matrix for following up on the implementation of decisions.

Finally, other meeting details, like equipment, materials, transportation, apparel, and food, should be addressed during the preparation phase.

2. Meeting

Some matters that deserve special consideration during the actual meeting are:

2.1 Structure

Meetings can be divided into sections for better efficiency, as follows:

a. *Opening*

During the opening phase, the group can perform a check-in, provide announcements, review the agenda, and follow up on items in progress.

b. *Development*

During the development phase, the group consults on action items and assigns responsibilities to the implementation of new decisions.

c. *Closing*

During the closing phase, the participants can perform a group review, begin drafting an agenda for the next meeting, and decide on issues like the date, time, and location of the next meeting.

2.2 Minutes

The group's recording secretary is responsible for taking the minutes of the meeting.

Aside from general information like group identification, attendees, absentees, location, date, and time, the only things that need to be recorded in the minutes are the background information that led to the decisions, the decisions, and complementary instructions, such as who is responsible for their execution, timelines for their completion, and what provisions should be used. Depending on the types of issues that a group deals with, a codification might be assigned to every decision for possible reference. It is up to each group to decide if other things should be recorded in the minutes as well.

Every time a decision with complementary instructions is recorded, it is good practice to read it aloud so that all can confirm its accuracy.

After a meeting is finished and the recording secretary has had the opportunity to review the draft of the minutes, the official minutes should be approved by the group and coded and filed for possible reference.

2.3 Decision-making

At the core of every meeting and its complementary phases is the decision-making process. However, because this matter is so substantial, it deserves a level of treatment that cannot be provided here. Perhaps it is sufficient to say that the mix of the collective individual understanding of diverse realities, including human reality, drives every group decision-making process. This mix determines intrapersonal, interpersonal, and group dynamics, and the result of every consideration.

Despite the weight of the collective mix, those with assigned roles can make singular contributions. A chairperson's contribution, in particular, can be significant enough to justify special training.

A chairperson has responsibilities such as mediating the order of the speakers when necessary, keeping the group focused on the topic of the moment, answering questions (with others' assistance if required), assisting with the testing of ideas, verbalizing the group's decisions to ensure that everyone is satisfied with them, and presenting decisions for voting in cases of a lack of consensus. Furthermore, the chairperson should at least be the person who cannot forget, in accordance with the adopted decision-making method, to consider the different phases of the process, ensuring that its basic principles are upheld, and wisely assisting individuals and the group to manifest the right qualities, attitude, and behavior called for by it.

3. Implementation of meeting decisions

    Unless a meeting is for something like learning or socialization to strengthen the group's culture, without a formal and methodical implementation phase of the decisions made, little of the effort spent during a meeting can generate results.

    Unfortunately, the challenge of this phase begins with a great number of meeting participants often distancing themselves from the execution of the decisions. The consequence is that the group's capacity to ensure good results becomes impaired. In the scope of group decision-making, decision and execution are split between the group and individuals. More precisely, the authority to make decisions rests with the group, while the power to implement them resides with individuals. There is no way out. Institutions cannot carry out decisions. The only way decisions can materialize is through individuals.

    To help mitigate this problem, groups can adopt the measure of appointing a second group member, the executive secretary in case there is one, to accompany and/or provide support to those members responsible for implementing individual decisions. An executive secretary can also serve as liaison to the group, keeping everybody abreast of the progress and organizing supplementary meetings if necessary. Of course, because decisions vary in importance, different levels of accompaniment are required for different categories of decisions.

9.3 Manuals

Using an organizational or administrative manual[3] solely as a reference guide can reinforce the perception that once one has learned one's job, nobody needs to pay further attention to it. This is especially true in circumstances where the practical work has morphed to a point that it outdates the instructions, making it difficult for managers to see the true potential of a manual as a management tool.

The fact is that an organizational manual is actually a collection of extremely important management documents, which does the following:

- Helps transpose subjective management work into objective work
- Helps integrate the organization, often by standardizing and streamlining certain aspects of the operations
- Facilitates review and improvement of operations
- Serves as training material
- Serves as one of the main repositories of organization memory – Not having manuals is like not having a backup of computer data, especially with certain critical organization knowledge

The point is that manuals should be used as tools for multiple purposes, instead of being viewed as management artifact of little value.

The way manuals are developed varies from organization to organization. Some organizations develop simple manuals, while others develop extremely detailed ones. This means that matters addressed in them can be very diverse, and specifications guiding their development can differ as well. For example, an organization might have a single manual with a single volume and only a few subjects with no major specification concerning their creation. On the other hand, another organization might have several manuals covering different systems, with each manual having diverse volumes covering different sub-systems. In turn, each volume has its collection of subjects and complementary information such as tables, catalogs, lists, and diagrams. In the latter case, good organization requires strict adherence to specifications such as formatting, identification, classification, codification, and index.

As such, manuals can be categorized into different types. Some examples are:

- Policy, Procedure, and Organizational
- Finance, HR, Operations, and so on (based on specializations)
- Planning, Provisioning, Organizing, Coordinating, and so forth (based on management functions)

Each type of document that is part of a manual should fall under the responsibility of a different management level. Depending on the characteristics of the organization, a single type could be utilized by more than one management level. The assignment of this responsibility should be specified in a document that, in turn, ends up itself being part of the manual. This document, which defines types of normative and mandate managerial decisions, establishes the norms and instructions on how to create manuals and other diverse documents.

The fact that in large and complex organizations manuals can be copious does not mean that small organizations cannot adjust the size of their manuals to fit their needs and capability to handle them. Small organizations should at least use a simple manual containing documents like current plan, basic policies, organizational chart, job descriptions, budgets, and some Operations info such as key processes, SOPs, blueprints, and formulas. It should also include lists of suppliers, products, and clients, or their database references.

Regardless of organization size, one measure that can contribute to the solution of the problem of keeping manuals current is the institution of precise periods of revisions for every document, with clearly assigned individuals responsible for this work—be they managers, direct reports, or both in a shared effort. For example, policies should be reviewed after the completion of every strategic planning phase. Job descriptions should be examined regularly at performance review sessions, prior to new hiring, and/or just prior to the launching of new strategic and operational plans.

In the final analysis, it is hard to sustain conventional excuses not to use manuals. The absence of manuals might well indicate that the organization is not very organized, does not have clear plans, and that processes are not well thought out.

9.4 Rewards & Penalties

In most places, local laws govern some of the rewards and penalties related to labor in organizational settings. Nevertheless, aside from such regulations, organizations, through their management, have some leeway, which they always use to complement matters not covered by those laws. Such complements exist in both formal and/or informal modes.

While the purpose of rewards is the reinforcement of positive behaviors, the goal of penalties is the restraining of illegitimate ones. To managers in particular, rewards and penalties are management tools to the extent that they induce adherence to mission, policies, plans, culture, and so forth. For the organization as a whole, these tools are critical for keeping the individual and collective interests in balance, serving, therefore, as "pillars of justice"[4]. Thus, by molding behavior, rewards and penalties are essential tools for dealing with the informal sphere of the organization.

Although managers are the ones usually creating and dispensing rewards and penalties, these undertakings are more appropriately carried out through collective efforts. After all, managers must also submit to the same system of rewards and penalties. In this regard, one particularly practical setup is that of a committee, which is especially indicated when addressing extraordinary behavioral issues. As mentioned before, the reason for such an approach is that through collective efforts, justice has a far better chance of being manifested.

In the absence of committees, assemblies, commissions and the like, managers should develop and carry out a reward and penalty system with the involvement of non-managers. The system must be formalized, and all members of the organization must be knowledgeable of the system. It must be noted that formalized systems should not take the format of countless regulations. In fact, the simpler the system is, the better it is.

Precautions must be taken against the incorrect use of rewards and penalties. If not correctly used, they can easily end up serving as instruments of injustice instead of justice. They must not be turned into tools of manipulation and displays of favoritism. How often are these tools used to increase productivity or dispensed with, neglecting the principle of equity? In other words, how often are rewards and penalties used to extract more work from people or to benefit some individuals and/or areas in detriment of others? The consequences of their misuse are the subversions of collaboration and unity.

In the end, the existence of collaborative and healthy work environments and, consequently the creation of real team spirit, are quite dependent on the correct utilization of these tools.

9.5 *Presentations*

Presentations[5] are not an obligatory tool for managers, but they can definitely be very helpful. Most managers occasionally, or even regularly, utilize this tool to address groups during day-to-day operations. Presentations can be formal or informal, and might include the assistance of media.

Presentations can be useful in many ways, some as simple as the sharing of information. However, their major contribution as a tool does not necessarily come from the sharing of content. Content can be delivered, for example, through a medium like a written report. Additionally, the way presentations are conveyed can serve as a good motivational tool, and, to the extent that attendance to them is open, they can strengthen organizational transparency. Nevertheless, these aspects of presentations are not the most relevant points either.

The main usefulness of presentations is the opportunity they offer for collective exploration of what is being shared. During presentations, or right after them, questions can be answered, weaknesses detected, solutions explored, and so on.

Among these explorations is a relatively rare opportunity for managers to gauge the staff's satisfaction with issues facing the organization and collectively address them.

The point is that many issues only become apparent to managers in a group environment. Some people, for instance, need to feel public support in order to have the courage to address uncomfortable matters. In this sense, from the manager's perspective, this aspect of presentations can become somewhat analogous to the handling of human dynamics in meetings. Of course, not all issues that surface during presentations can be fully addressed on the spot. Cases involving personal problems are good examples of issues that are best handled in private.

Sometimes problems that surface during the course of a presentation may in fact be issues not directly related to the topic at hand. Occasionally diagnoses may be necessary, and unexpected solutions adopted in order to address the real problem. A very simple example is the quite common and unfair complaints that financial presentations are not clear enough. The truth is that there are realistic limits on how much one can simplify a financial presentation without compromising content. In this example, the problem and the solution are to be found in the level of financial knowledge that those having to deal with such a subject must necessarily possess. It has nothing to do with the numbers being presented. Regardless, managers must robustly back their presentations with facts if they expect to minimize the risk of presentations being derailed.

The opportunity for collective participation with their substantial benefits should be significant enough to motivate managers to develop the necessary skills—that is, preparation, delivery, and consultation—to use presentations.

9.6 Application Software

Application software is created for an infinite number of purposes, but software that directly concerns management can be categorized as follows:

a.   Applications that serve as tools, even if presented as management functions

- Personal manager assistants such as Outlook and Entourage, which include functionalities like calendars, journals, email, task management, and so forth
- Applications for Planning, Organizing, Provisioning, Coordinating, and so on
- Mind mapping software

b.   Applications designed to serve as Management Programs (for Management Programs, see chapter 10)

- Customer Relationship Management (CRM)
- Human Resource Management Systems (HRMS)
- Product Data Management (PDM)
- Business Technology Management (BTM)
- Decision Support System (DSS)
- Enterprise Content Management (ECM)
- Enterprise Resource Planning (ERP)
- Geographic Information System (GIS)
- Groupware and Collaborative Systems (G&CS)
- Integrated Workplace Management System (IWMS)
- Material Requirements Planning (MRP)

- Product Lifecycle Management (PLM)
- Project Management (PM)
- Strategic Enterprise Management (SEM)
- Supply Chain Management (SCM)
- Virtual Management (VM)

Some advantages of application software for management purposes are:

a. They can help with self-organization
b. They can help increase the span of direct management
c. They tend to incorporate best practices of rules, organizations, processes, and so forth

9.7 Other Management Tools

Like many other subjects in management, the classification of tools is quite difficult. Three major hindrances to classifying them are:

1. *A single tool can be used for more than one purpose* – For example, an interview can be used for monitoring, provisioning, or problem solving.

2. *Not all features of a tool are useful for categorizing it, though some might place it into a sub-classification* – This usually happens when differences in features do not point to anything beyond variations in the format of a tool. For example, financial reports can be presented through financial statements, charts, and written reports. In other cases, variations are so minor that even the basic format of the presentation is the same, like in line graphs with or without marks or in 3D.

3. *Some things can barely be classified as tools* – Some are more like concepts, and others are more like methods.

Whatever the case may be, the following arrangement might broaden one's view of the management tools[6] out there and possibly serve as a basic reference.

Analytical
- ABC Analysis (Activity Based Cost)

- Cost-benefit Analysis
- Financial Ratios
- Force Field Analysis
- Interview
- Pick Chart
- Quantitative Marketing Research
- Questionnaire
- SWOT Analysis

Audits
- Environmental
- Financial
- Information Systems
- Processes
- Quality
- Security
- Social Responsibility
- Strategic

Charts
- Bar Charts
- Bubble Charts
- Control Chart
- Gantt Chart
- Normal Probability Plots
- Organizational Chart
- Pareto Chart
- Pie Charts
- Radar Charts
- Run Charts
- Scatter Plots

Diagrams
- Affinity Diagram
- Cause and Effect Diagrams
  - Fishbone
  - Interrelationship Diagraph
  - Tree Diagram

- Critical to Quality tree (CTQ tree)
- Eisenhower Diagram
- House of Quality
- Matrix Diagram
- Process Decision Program Chart
- Relations Diagram
- TOWS

Forecasting
- Failure Mode and Effects Analysis
- Scenario Planning
- "What If" Scenarios
- Cash Flow

Monitoring
- Balanced Scorecard
- Check Sheet
- Financial Statements
- Logs
- Observation
- Table of Responsibility
- Team Action Items
- Written Reports

Problem Solving
- 5 Whys
- Brainstorm
- De Bono – Six Thinking Hats
- Questioning – What, Why, When, Where, Whom, How
- Root Cause Analysis (diagram)
- TRIZ – Theory of Inventive Problem Solving

Process
- Activity Network Diagrams
- Checklist
- Flowchart
- Forms
- Prioritization Matrix

- Process Boundaries
- Process Capability
- Process Mapping
- SIPOC Analysis (Suppliers, Inputs, Process, Outputs, Customers)
- Work Breakdown Structure

Statistical
- Analysis of Variance
- Correlation
- Design of Experiments
- Pareto Analysis
- Regression Analysis
- Stratification
- Taguchi Methods

Work Measurement
- Analytical Estimating
- Benchmarking
- Method Study
- Performance Measurement
- Performance Rating
- Pre-determined Motion-time Systems
- Standard Data
- Time-motion Study
- Work Sampling (statistic)

10

Management Programs

Simply put, Management Programs are customized methods for carrying out part of, one of, or several management functions.

The production of literature that can be placed under this category seems to be almost as abundant as the invention of new deliverables. It might even be plausible to say that the title *Management Programs* encompasses the largest ongoing percentage of knowledge generated in the field of management. While some programs turn out to be just fads, others prove their worth by undergoing improvements and spurring variations that endure for considerable periods.

These programs, which might or might not be methodically grounded on fundamental management principles, are the result of efforts intended to address daily management issues. In any case, all of them end up customizing part of, one of, or several management functions as they tackle particular management concerns.

To help make sense of this large body of knowledge, some categorizations that might be used, depending on the program's extensiveness, are the following:

- *Punctual Programs* – This category might be used to indicate small management programs, which in some cases could better be referred to as techniques. Programs in this category do not attempt to cover even a full single function. Instead, they address very particular issues that a specific function has to deal with.

- *Functional Management Programs* – This category might include customized methods developed to try to address whole management functions, like Monitoring, Planning, or Supporting.

- *Comprehensive Management Programs* – This category might include broad schemes that try to cover several or all management functions at once. These programs are not necessarily intended to address issues of single functional areas. In fact, they often try to cover multiple areas or even the entire organization.

Beyond dealing with management functions and covering diverse work domains, many management programs provide useful tools and rules. Some also address personal qualities relevant to management, and even philosophies of work.

In the same way that programs might not be developed with a focus on fundamental management principles, managers who make use of them might not be conscious of the fact that they are implementing such principles. In any case, by employing management programs, managers make use of "blueprints" that guide them through the discharge of their duties under specific contexts. Hence, programs facilitate managers' lives by helping them overcome an occasional lack of familiarity and/or adherence to basic management concepts.

Although it is very valuable to learn management programs, sole reliance on them is never enough. The main reason is that no management program, or a combination of them, can ever cover all the needs of an area. Managers should have the capacity to execute their functions without the assistance of management programs. Furthermore, a solid command of management principles can empower managers to develop their own customized programs, allowing them, for instance, to tackle new situations from scratch.

The following are examples of management programs:

- Complaint Management
- Concurrent or Simultaneous Engineering (CE or SE)
- Constraint Management
- Continuous Improvement (CI)
- Cost Management
- Crisis Management
- Critical Management Studies
- Customer Relationship Management
- Data Management
- Design Management
- Earned Value Management
- Hot Desking
- Integration Management
- Just-in-time
- Lean Management
- Knowledge Management
- Management by Coaching and Development (MBCD)
- Management by Objectives (MBO)
- Management by Organizational Development (MBOD)
- Management by Performance (MBP)
- Management by Walking Around (MBWA)
- Management by Work Simplification (MBWS)
- Merge Management
- Performance Management
- Product Lifecycle Management
- Quality Function Deployment (QFD)
- Quality Management
- Reliability-Centered Maintenance (RCM)
- Systems Management
- Team Management
- Total Productive Maintenance (TPM)
- Total Quality Management (Programs like Six Sigma, Quality Circles, Kaizen-Atarimae Hinshitsu-Kansei-Miryokuteki Hinshitsu)
- Value Engineering (VE), and Risk Management

The following four management programs could easily be on the list of the top programs that all managers should master:

a. Strategic Management
b. Budget Management
c. Change Management
d. Project Management

10.1 Strategic Management

One way to better appreciate the value of a strategic management[1] program might be through the realization that it is in the category of programs that undergo improvements over time. Table 10.1.a shows the evolution of strategic management through four phases.

Phases of Strategic Evolution

Phase 1 Basic Financial Planning	Manager initiates serious planning when requested to propose next year's budget.
Phase 2 Forecast-based Planning	Annual budgets become less useful at simulating long-term planning; managers attempt to propose 5-year plans.
Phase 3 Externally Oriented Planning (strategic planning)	Frustrated with highly political and ineffectual 5-year plans, top managers take control of planning process by initiating *strategic planning*.
Phase 4 Strategic Management	There is an involvement of a greater number of lower level managers and non-managers from various departments and work groups. They develop and integrate a series of strategic plans aimed at achieving the company's primary objectives. Strategic plans now detail the implementation, evaluation, and control issues.

Table 10.1.a – *WHEELEN, THOMAS L., HUNGER, J. DAVID, STRATEGIC MANAGEMENT AND BUSINESS POLICY, 8th Edition, © 2002. Adapted by permission of Pearson Education, Inc., Upper Saddle River, NJ.*

The evolution of this management program seems to have been guided mainly by the search for ways to expand the considerations needed for the development of better (strategic) plans. As seen above, the first attempt at improvement focused on the expansion of the period covered by the plans. Later, a move was made towards broadening environmental scanning in order to improve situational analysis. Eventually, the door was opened to increasing the number of personnel involved with strategic planning, further helping the operational staff to implement the strategy.

With the aid of such a strategic management program, strategic plans can now be unfolded in a more methodical way throughout the organization, thus increasing overall organizational strategic alignment and efficiency.

Table 10.1.b graphically portrays a strategic cycle with its unfolding steps.

Overview of a Strategic Management Unfoldment Cycle (Table 10.1.b)

Wheelen, Thomas L., Hunger, J. David, Strategic Management and business policy, 8th Edition, © 2002, p. 1. Adapted by permission of Pearson Education, Inc., Upper Saddle.

10.1.1 Strategy

A strategy is a carefully designed scheme, or plan, intended to increase the chances of achieving a specific objective in the face of a complex state of affairs. A strategy itself might be simple or complex, and it can be designed to be carried out over the course of a specified timeline that can vary from short to long term. For example, a strategy might be developed to bid on an important contract or to guide an organization through a long-term modernization process. The effort put into the development of a strategy depends on factors like the institutional knowledge to create one, financial resources for doing so, the manager's personality, or the effectiveness of a strategic design committee's consultation.

In any case, the main factor to be kept in mind regarding strategy is that the process of formulating it, and often of implementing it as well, is much more complex than that of ordinary plans.

Faced with such circumstances, wisdom calls for the dedication of great effort toward broadening one's vision concerning all the factors that could influence the proposed strategy. This implies extensive information gathering, considerable analysis, and diligence in searching for the best course, all of which can rarely be accomplished in a single day. Perhaps the only thing more risky than strategies formulated in one day are those devised solely on the feelings of single managers. Certainly, intuition has its merits, and in some circumstances it might be the only alternative, but to rely exclusively on a single manager's intuition can result in a strategy that is not as well thought out as one developed by multiple individuals consulting together.

Strategy concerned with the overall operation of an organization is so important that many consider it the most significant determinant for the success or failure of the enterprise. Using the analogy of warfare, a successful strategy is one that should allow even the weakest army to win a conflict. One example of an occasionally successful strategy adopted by some new market entrants has been to serve markets that are ignored by better-established organizations. Once these latter entrants acquire a reasonable size, they move on to participate in the most prized markets, eventually becoming major players.

It is important to understand that the definition of strategic objectives alone is insufficient to create the conditions for attaining success. Unfortunately, it is somewhat common to pursue "strategic objectives" without ever developing plans to implement them. Strategic Objectives provide directions, but do not provide clear steps for accomplishing the intended goals.

For example, the owners of a business retail store who want to grow their operation see three possible routes for reaching their goal: the increase in floor space, the opening of another branch, and the set up of an online store. After considering several variables, the owners conclude that they can only afford to pursue one of the three options at first, so they make the choice to open a new branch. At this point, the owners believe that they have created a strategy, but in reality, they have only defined a strategic objective. Nevertheless, without a strategy, the owners simply start scouting for what they believe to be a suitable location for the new store, relying on monetary savings to duplicate the first store's experience. If the owners had created a strategic plan (and an operational plan), however, they could have established the appropriate marketing mix for the new branch, created a cash flow projection to support the project, and addressed tactical issues, such as when to enter the new marketplace, how to determine which suppliers are most important, and how to secure those suppliers.

To increase the chances of success, strategic objectives must be fully supported by strategies or strategic plans.

Strategic plans must provide overall explanations for how strategic objectives should be achieved, indicating such things as the organization's strengths to be used, weaknesses to be remedied, opportunities to be explored, and threats to be addressed, as per SWOT[2] (Strengths, Weaknesses, Opportunities, and Threats) analysis. Because well-executed strategic planning relies on so many external factors and requires so much effort, and because the implementation of the plan takes so long, strategic plans are generally intended for the long-term.

Although strategic plans developed by top-level management (with or without general participation) are usually relatively simple, they are essential as the first step in the overall organizational planning process. For instance, strategic plans can be formulated by simply pairing the factors specified in the SWOT analysis using a matrix called TOWS. The idea is to use one factor of the SWOT to address another. For example, strengths are used to address weaknesses, and opportunities are used to address threats. The detail of the strategic plan is completed by cascading and unfolding the strategic plan through the other management levels. The correct unfolding of strategic plans throughout all other management levels is extremely important for attaining success. If correctly done, an organization becomes strategically aligned, ensuring the unification of efforts. Only then can a strategy be expected to influence a whole organization.

Here is an example of an unfolding strategic process:

Top-Level Management

Top-level management carries out the strategic planning, which includes more than just the definition of strategic objectives or even the design of a plan.

At this level, most of the effort is dedicated to steps leading to the formulation of the plan:

- Comprehension of the complexity of the situation at hand
- Revision of the mission, in keeping with the present reality
- Development of vision(s)
- Development of strategic objective(s)
- Exploration of alternative plans before one is selected

Consequently, the plan document presents more subjects than just the strategic plan. It might include:

- Situational analysis with key environmental indicators
- Restated or redefined mission, accompanied by a statement about the organizational culture to be nurtured
- Vision(s) of the future state of the organization
- Strategic objectives
- Strategic plan
- List of available and desired key personnel and resources
- Appendix
    - Organizational chart, at least the top part of the structure
    - Policies
    - Job descriptions of key personnel

Middle- and Lower-Levels Management

Middle- and lower-levels managers use the strategic plan document to develop their operational plans.

Before starting plan formulation, they:

- Study the strategic plan document
- Perform additional operational analysis
- Explore alternative plans before selecting one

The operational plan document might include:

- Vision(s) of the future state of sizeable work areas
- Operational objectives for business units, functional areas
- Operational plan describing major processes, activities, programs, or projects, along a timeline with required provisions, including assigned functions and values linked to respective work to be done
- Budget, which is the conversion of the operational plan into financial language
- Operational performance indicators, aside from budget, with the help of a tool like Balanced Scorecard
- Appendix
    - Key guidelines
    - Detailed organizational chart
    - *What-if* budgets
    - Contingency plans

Table 10.1.1 shows strategic considerations of for-profit organizations distributed through three administrative levels.

Corporate, Business Unit and Functional Area Strategies

Strategy	Primary Concern	Particular Consideration
Corporate Strategy - Top-Level Management (Board of Directors and Top Executives)	Core Competency	• Customer Intimacy • Operational Excellence • Product Leadership

	Directional[3]	• Growth
		  ▪ Concentration
		    ○ Horizontal
		    ○ Vertical
		  ▪ Diversification
		    ○ Concentric
		    ○ Conglomerate
		• Stability
		  ▪ Pause/proceed with caution
		  ▪ No change
		  ▪ Profit
		• Retrenchment
		  ▪ Turnaround
		  ▪ Captive Company
		  ▪ Sell-Out/Divestment
		• Bankruptcy/Liquidation

	Business Unit Portfolio[4]	• Heartland • Edge-of-heartland • Ballast • Alien Territory • Value Trap
Business Unit Strategy - Top/Mid-level Management (Business Executives)	Product Portfolio[5]	• Cash Cow • Star • Dog • Question Mark
	Cooperative Strategy	• Collusion • Alliance
	Competitive Strategy[6]	• Differentiation • Segmentation • Cost
Functional Strategy - Mid/Lower-Level Management	Functional Area	• Operations • Personnel • Marketing • Finance • Information Technology • Other

Table 10.1.1

The following is an example of the unfolding of a strategy based on the model above:

1. **Top-level Management** – After a careful diagnosis, the board of directors and top executives decide that the *corporation* should work towards Stability over the next 5 years. To achieve stability, the organization should strengthen its core competency of Customer Intimacy. Furthermore, it should let go of companies with a poor cultural fit (Parenting-Fit-Ballast, Value Trap, and Alien Territory) with the corporation culture.

2. **Middle-level Management** – In order to accomplish these objectives, *business unit* executives decide to concentrate only on products that are well established and are generating cash (Portfolio-Cash Cow), and on products that are on the rise (Portfolio-Star). Additionally, business units should engage in Cooperative Strategy-Alliance with organizations entertaining complementary interests.

3. **Lower-level Management** – *Functional area* management decides on Marketing, Personnel, Financial, and IT strategies to support the strategic plans of the corporate and business units.

Concisely speaking,

1. **Corporate Strategy** addresses core competency, directional and business portfolio issues

2. **Business Unit Strategy** addresses industry issues

3. **Functional Strategy** addresses functional areas issues

In organizations with fewer management levels, the strategic planning responsibilities of the missing higher hierarchies fall on what is the top management level of the simpler organizational structure. For instance, the top management of an organization that is comprised of a single business unit (not a conglomerate) takes on responsibilities that are applicable to both corporate and business unit strategies, as shown in the example above. In some cases, especially in small and mid-sized organizations, top management might end up taking over the responsibility of functional strategy as well.

10.2 Budget Management

Budget management[7], or budgeting, is one of the most important management programs that exists. It is so important that all managers at all levels must make use of it. It is not without reason that so many people have, throughout history, acknowledged its worth and recognized its connection with planning. As the saying goes, "Not to budget is not to plan".

The rationale for the connection between the budget and the plan rests on the fact that numbers form a universal language, and money is a universal equivalent. In other words, budgets are plans expressed in monetary language, and by extension, budgeting can be equivalent to planning.

As such, budgets should be viewed as financial translations of plans, with the added bonus, due to their universal equivalence, of being able to consolidate the organization's diverse plans into a single plan. They are not a perfect translation, in part because during the conversion, some details are always added and adjustments are sometimes made.

Budgets are also very effective because they greatly help with the following:

- *Plan implementation* – Unlike a great number of organizational plans, budgets render themselves to higher levels of detailing and precision. To achieve those ends, monetary figures should be allocated to specific accounts and result centers along a timeline, e.g. per fiscal year, quarterly, semiannually, and/or some other specified period. For instance, if someone from the Finance Department plans to go on a business trip in October, the line item "travel" and the result center "Finance Department" must be reflected in "October" with the expenses of $1,200.00 related to the trip. This means that, in accordance with the plan, the amount must not be spread throughout the fiscal year. For example, one must not allocate $100.00 per month as if one does not know when the trip is supposed to take place. To budget like the latter example is the same as saying that there is no plan, that the trip can occur at any time.

  Let us suppose that, for lack of adherence to what has been planned, October has passed and the person did not travel. However, because there are always other things happening, in November the organization is embarking on the conversion of its financial system, as scheduled for the turn of the year. The result is that by disregarding the plan, consequences start to accumulate: now the person has to choose between participating in the conversion to the new system or going on the intended business trip, because they cannot do both. If, for example, the choice is to go on the important business trip, the person might now have to face a higher travel season with higher airfare tickets and lodging costs, completely booked hotels, leaving the department under-staffed, and so on. In the end, part of the plan can no longer be accomplished, and what might be done can easily end up going over budget.

The lesson is that before moving ahead with any task or activity, one must refer to the appropriate budget and then act accordingly. Managers should not use budgets just to compare what took place (actual) versus what has been budgeted (projected). Instead, they must also use budgets proactively as a plan that must be followed. Doing so significantly reduces or eliminates the gap between actual and budgeted, between reality and plan.

- *Plan monitoring* – As mentioned before, all transactions that have financial value have to be recorded on a daily basis using accounting principles, due to either government imposition and/or good management. This makes accounting the broadest and one of the most accurate forms of recording the day-to-day operation of any type of organization. Hence, by comparing what is being recorded against what has been budgeted, it is possible to obtain a picture of how the implementation of the plan is progressing.

- *Liaising* – Due to the qualities discussed above, budgets are an excellent instrument for informing others on the progress of a plan, and for motivating people towards its completion.

Furthermore, as all financial statements represent the same principle of translating operation into numbers (monetary language), budgets can take on any of their formats. For example:

- Balance Sheet Budget
- Income Statement / P&L Budget
- Cash Flow Budget

- Capital Investment Budget

Regarding budget design, it is primarily the type of functional area that determines what method* should be used. Some of the methods include:

- *Output/input* (not input/output) – Used by areas that generate revenue.
- *Top-down* – Used by support areas that have quite consistent deliverables throughout time. Examples include Finance and Personnel.
- *Bottom-up* – Used by areas that have to rethink their deliverables every new budgeting cycle. For example, Marketing and IT

10.3 Change Management

Since, on the one hand, movement and change are laws of nature, and, on the other hand, our social reality depends on this physical world for its manifestation, organizations are not and cannot be insulated from such laws. As much as many would like to keep things unchangeable, the reality is that it is just not possible. This, however, does not mean that changes in organizations cannot be managed. Indeed, they can and should be. In this regard, it is important to note that the change referred to here is not the kind of change that occurs almost imperceptibly, but rather that class of change that happens in strenuous ways, producing noticeable distinctions between different states. Strenuous changes can be categorized as sought and as unexpected.

One of the main differences between the management of these two types of strenuous changes is that changes that are sought can be planned under comfortable conditions, while changes that are unexpected require plans to be, if possible, carried out in haste. Changes that are sought allow for more methodical improvements, which minimize unavoidable disruptions. This approach is very useful, for example, when seeking technological innovations. Although it is not possible to come up with a list of what needs to be tracked in order to be prepared for unexpected change, the best way to go about addressing it is by being proactive in constantly scanning the internal and external environments for the first signs of instabilities. In any

---

* Although each type of functional area uses primarily one method, areas might use additional methods to budget for particular accounts or result centers.

case, every time strenuous changes are identified or sought, managers should develop and implement targeted interventions.

Furthermore, categories of change such as major and minor are used to help split the responsibility between different management levels. Almost without exception, major changes, which might focus on re-organizing and/or redirecting an entire organization, are top-level managers' responsibility. Of course, during a process of large-scale change, all managers, from top to lower levels, should become involved, but top managers are still the ones spearheading the process. This type of change should take place very sporadically because, among other things, it tends to be costly, risky, and takes much more time to plan and implement. On the other hand, lower level managers might manage minor or incremental changes, which are smaller in scope and should happen more frequently. The reason is that the pace of operational dynamics is much faster at a lower level. If issues like customer dissatisfaction, technical modifications and training of personnel are to be efficiently addressed, they need to happen quickly and preferably with the assistance of a Change Management[8] program.

As expected, mission and strategy must guide all change, however minor. For example, if a small step in the production process of a sports car is elected for change in order to cut cost, it can only happen if the change does not compromise the organization's mission of extreme speed.

Some inducers of changes may be:

- Change of strategy
- Consumers' demand
- Ecological demand
- Major stakeholders' change of heart
- Market adjustment
- Organizational merge
- Personnel turnover
- Societal demand
- Technological innovation

To help managers tackle change in a methodical way, subject-based classifications are also used. Again, there is no standardization for the words used for these classifications. This problem sometimes results in different schools and practitioners adopting different words to express similar intent.

At other times, one or more of these classifications can be seen in contexts not related to change. In any case, some possible classifications are:

- Incremental and Transformational Interventions
- Small, Medium, and Large-scale Interventions
- Strategic and Techno-structural Interventions
- Management Development, Team Development, and Group Process Interventions

Classification could also be based on management functions such as:

- Provisioning (resources and personnel) Interventions
- Organizing Interventions
- Coordinating Interventions
- Cultural Interventions

Three major changing models are:

- Lewin's Model
- Action Research Model
- The Positive Change Model

Simply by using the framework provided by Lewin's model, which has many variations, one can achieve wonderful results. The framework comes from Lewin's work[9] on group dynamics, which outlines three different phases for changing processes: Unfreeze, Move, and Freeze. Although this characterization of the different stages is extremely helpful, a modest observation could be made in relation to the expression freeze. Because resistance to change is common, the expression might unintentionally feed this behavior, which should be eliminated. As an alternative, the phases related to modern change management could perhaps be renamed to something like Preparation, Transition, and Adaptation.

Under each of these phases, a number of factors should be considered, such as:

Preparation

- Diagnosis and analysis, not forgetting to identify and classify stakeholders
- Involvement of as many people as possible, creating response to change

- Creation of change management structure, if appropriate
- Initiation of the process of keeping as many people as possible informed throughout all steps[*]
- Development of plan, not forgetting to create vision
- Handling of resistance to change
- Provisions needed to carry out the change

Transition

- Coordination of the implementation process, especially sticking to the schedule
- Monitoring of provisions connected to implementation

Adaptation

- Monitoring of new state based on new measurements
- Supporting, including further training if necessary
- Cultural Modeling, with cultural adjustment if necessary

10.4 Project Management

A *project* can be defined as a one-time endeavor with the goal of producing one or more deliverables. These deliverables can be for intermediary or final consumption. For example, a project might deliver a factory that, as an intermediary product, is used for the creation of other goods, while the construction of a customized yacht is an example of final consumption.

In any organization, including one that does not engage in projects for the production of deliverables for final consumption, one-time endeavors are also very much a fact of life. From the research and development of new products to projects, such as factory expansion, organization or office redesign, or implementation of new technology, projects play a frequent and essential role in the lives of organizations.

Because this program is solidly grounded on very practical tools, the effects of its role on production are more apparent than for most programs. This characteristic makes the contribution of a manager more discernible.

---

[*] One of the worst things that can be done in a change process is to lack transparency, leaving people uninformed.

The following are some different approaches to project management[10], each suited to specific contexts or needs:

- Agile Project
- Critical Chain Project
- Event Chain Methodology
- Extreme Project
- PRINCE2
- PRiSM
- Process-based
- Traditional

Regardless of the approach, a great portion of the Project Management program is focused on coordination. Of course, Planning, Organizing and Provisioning are also integral parts of the program, as are the complementary management functions.

The life cycle of a project could contain the following phases:

1. Feasibility Study
2. Design
3. Production
4. Delivery or Start-up

Additionally, the program could have a monitoring phase for possible adjustments before complete delivery, which might include restarting the project if necessary.

Each of these phases can, and should, be broken down into sub-phases, and each of these sub-phases might have specific considerations, knowledge, tools, or procedures associated with them.

Furthermore, since projects often cause strenuous changes, managers should also utilize a change management program to support such endeavors.

In summary, as there are plenty of situations during ongoing operations for which project management expertise can be very useful, and the benefits of its utilization are very significant, managers have a lot to gain by incorporating this management program into their skill set.

11

Managers' Functional Areas of Expertise

Functional areas are specialized areas of collective production, often with a sufficient number of personnel and complexity of processes to accommodate individuals dedicated exclusively to managerial work.

Although it is extremely helpful for a manager to have knowledge of the non-managerial work performed in a functional area, or in fact, in any area under his or her responsibility, such knowledge is not intrinsic to the discipline of management. The relation of management to different work areas is equivalent to that of management to management levels—that is, management functions are the same in all areas regardless of variations in the non-managerial work being performed. For example, if an organization has Sales and Accounting Departments, the non-managerial knowledge of each area is, of course, different even though the managerial knowledge to be used in both areas is the same.

The inspiration for using the knowledge of the operation of functional areas for the preparation of managers may have come from:

- The realization of the importance of some functional areas to all organizations
- The eventual need for functional areas to have dedicated management
- The importance of non-managerial knowledge to management

Even though this solution appears to be almost a full package, during the theoretical design of management courses, non-managerial work seems to have taken center stage. At its core, the rationale guiding the development of such courses seems to be based on the notion that if a person knows how an area should function, especially if such knowledge is derived from best practices for the area, he or she should be able to manage it. This reasoning also appears to be endorsed by the common practice of promoting people to their first managerial position based primarily on their non-managerial expertise. Nevertheless, it is often widely recognized that individuals who are promoted for the first time to a managerial position are unsure of what they should do as managers. It is also true that complaints are common about most management courses not being able to adequately prepare individuals for the real world. To be fair, management courses address other subjects besides non-managerial knowledge. However, when they focus on what managers are supposed to do, they often do so implicitly through management programs. In the end, students leave managerial courses without being able to clearly distinguish between managerial and non-managerial work. In spite of such limitations, organizations still function largely because they are not dependent on single individuals or even single managers.

To evaluate a manager's state of preparedness, a quick look at the following categorizations might be helpful:

State 1 – *Manager lacks relevant managerial knowledge but possess good non-managerial expertise* – At first, this state seems to be destined to fail. The reason is that in non-managerial expertise there is very little intrinsic knowledge that allows for the facilitation of piecing multiple work areas together and assisting with their collective functioning. To succeed, at some point along the way, managers in this state must be able to incorporate managerial knowledge into their work. A manager should at least be able to grasp some of the basics of management on his own through keen insight and sensibility, have the capacity to maintain what has been inherited for as long as possible, and/or have the sagacity to tap into other people's potential. An example of this is an engineer who becomes a good manager without ever studying management theories.

State 2 – *Manager possesses good managerial knowledge but lacks significant non-managerial expertise* – This state is far from being ideal, but it has a better chance of succeeding than State 1. At least both ingredients, managerial and non-managerial, are present in the work area. However, here the path to success is also conditioned on the manager's capacity to tap into the potential of others, particularly through the involvement of direct reports. An example is a manager who is able to successfully shift from one industry to another.

State 3 – *Manager lacks both significant managerial and non-managerial knowledge* – Strange as it might seem, this state too can exist for a certain period as long as, of course, one is capable of putting other people's potential to use. With an increase in complexity, however, managers in this state must acquire managerial knowledge, or they will end up endangering the organization. An example of this would be that of a successful entrepreneur who tries several different types of businesses until something works.

State 4 – *Manager possesses solid managerial and non-managerial knowledge* – Obviously, this is the ideal state. The necessity for both kinds of knowledge can be observed in the fact that management functions exist to address non-managerial work. How, for example, can a plan be created without knowledge of the work that needs to be carried out?

In the end, the correlation between managerial and non-managerial work has to be obtained in one way or another. The two have to come together either through a manager's acquisition of expertise in both or through a partnership with direct reports.

It can be helpful to note that the proportion of such a correlation can fluctuate some with the change in managerial level. The lower the level is, the greater the need for non-managerial knowledge. As one moves up, such knowledge becomes less relevant. While at high management levels managers can rely on other managers, at lower levels managers have to deal directly with non-managers handling non-managerial work. It is also quite common at lower levels for managers to be faced with circumstances where new direct reports are less knowledgeable about the non-managerial work that needs to be done than they are. To address this situation in a way that reduces a manager's involvement with non-managerial work, it is possible to create conditions where direct reports teach and support each other.

Managers benefit from knowing their own areas, but they and the organization benefit even more if they have a basic understanding of other areas. Every manager needs some knowledge of Finance, Personnel, IT, and so forth, both to improve the performance of his or her area and to better integrate it with the rest of the organization. Such an expansion of knowledge might also be useful as preparation for assuming higher managerial positions.

11.1 Specialist

The term specialist, in contrast to generalist, refers to the proficiency of an individual in a specific work area, possibly evolving to become an expert in a specific industry.

Because the level of complexity of a single area can vary enough that it requires the creation of sub-areas, it is feasible to have specialist managers at all levels. For instance, depending on the size of an organization, a Finance Department might have specialist managers in top, middle and lower level positions. In this example, a CFO occupies the top position, a Controller and a Treasurer would be the middle managers, and the heads of Accounts Receivable, Accounts Payable, Budgeting, and so forth, are the lower-level managers.

Some of the main areas of specialization are Operations, Marketing, Finance, Human Affairs (Resources), and Information Technology. These areas should be present in almost all organizations. Other areas, like Legal, General Services and/or Facilities, which may include sub-areas for Infrastructure, Cleaning, and Security, are areas that are added to an organization depending on characteristics such as size, type, complexity, and outreach.

Below is an overview for each of these main areas of specialization.

11.1.1 Operations

Operations[1] is the area of an organization where the final collective deliverables take shape.

As expected, Operations vary in the same proportion as the number of organizations and types of deliverables. Consequently, the execution of management functions, choice of programs to use, adoption of approach, and selected tools can be adapted for each organization.

Depending on the size of the organization, other areas directly associated with Operations are Research and Development, Quality Control, and Marketing. All other areas are generally considered supporting areas.

The focus of Operations can be divided into three groups, with specialized and/or supplementary areas, such as:

1. Obtention (Procurement)
   - Raw-material
   - Inventory
   - Research and Development (R&D)

2. Production
   - "Industrial processes"
   - Quality Control
   - Maintenance

3. Distribution
   - Distribution Channels
   - Logistics and Transportation

Some of the main concerns driving Operations are:

- How should deliverables be produced?
   - Which provisions should be used?
   - Which processes are necessary?
   - How should facilities be laid out?
   - What technologies should be adopted?
   - How can quality of deliverables be improved?

- o   What must be done to ensure cost efficiency?
- How can constant supply be ensured?
- How can the supply chain be improved?
- How much inventory should be carried?
- How can distribution be improved?

A great deal of focus is on efficiency. Therefore, Operations Management often includes substantial measurement and analysis of processes.

11.1.2 Marketing

Marketing[2] is an admirable area, when carried out ethically. It helps connect demand with offer, deliverables with clients and, as such, is extremely important to any organization.

A few fundamental Marketing concepts are mentioned below from *Kellogg on Marketing*, 2001:

- "Companies *sell* products; companies *market* brands." (Bobby J. Calder and Steven J. Reagan, p. 58)

- "To *market*, we have to go beyond the product. We must transcend whatever the product is as a physical or objective entity. We must create and convey the meaning of the product." (Bobby J. Calder and Steven J. Reagan, p. 58)

- "Meaning is more than description or wordsmithing... Meaning is the idea of the thing. Whatever the product *is*, meaning is how it is to be understood from the consumer's perspective." (Bobby J. Calder and Steven J. Reagan, p. 59)

- "Meaning is the stuff of brands." (Bobby J. Calder and Steven J. Reagan, p. 59)

- "...rather than *giving* customers what they want... strategies are increasingly designed to help buyers *learn* what they want." (Gregory S. Carpenter, Rashi Glazer, and Kent Nakamoto, p. 103)

The *Targeting and Positioning Statement* is a basic guiding tool that should be created by the Marketing Department and used by other areas of the organization as well. This statement should contain the answer for the following questions (Kellogg, 2001, Alice M. Tybout and Brian Sternthall, pages 51-54):

1. Who should be targeted for brand use?
2. When should the brand be considered (that is, what goal does the brand allow the target to achieve?)
3. Why should the brand be chosen over other alternatives in the competitive set?
4. How will choosing the brand help the target accomplish his or her goal(s)?

Some of the main concerns driving the area are:

- Which segment should be targeted?
- What should our main competency be?
  - Operational Excellence
  - Customer Intimacy
  - Product Leadership
- What type of brand shall we have?
  - Functional
  - Image
  - Experiential
- What deliverables should be produced?
- What should the prices of the deliverables be?
- How much of each deliverable should be produced?
- How should the chosen segment be targeted?
  - How should the brand be marketed?
- How should the deliverables be promoted?
- How should the deliverables be distributed?
- How should the organization keep up with changes in the targeted segment?
- What is needed to develop and launch new deliverables?

Table 11.1.2 presents a list of elements that should be addressed by each of the four Ps (Product, Place, Promotion, and Price) that compose Marketing's main variables.

4Ps – Marketing Mix Variables[3]

Product	Place	Promotion	Price
Quality	Channels	Advertising	List price
Features	Coverage	Personal Selling	Discounts
Options	Locations	Sales Promotion	Allowances
Style	Inventory	Publicity	Payment Periods
Brand Name	Transport		Credit Items
Packing			
Sizes			
Services			
Warranties			
Returns			

Table 11.1.2 – *KOTLER, PHIL, MARKETING MANAGEMENT: ANALYSIS, PLANNING, AND CONTROL, 4th edition, © 1980, p. 89. Reprinted by permission of Pearson Education, Inc., Upper Saddle River, NJ.*

Core Marketing activities, most of which can be used as criteria for departmentalization, often include:

- Brand Management
- Market Research / Consumer Behavior
- Product Development (in conjunction with Operations)
- Pricing (in conjunction with Finance and Operations)
- Promotion – Publicity (free) / Advertising (paid)
- Sales (Brick & Mortar / E-commerce)
- Client / Customer Relations

Complementary activities can include:

- Public Relations (PR)
- Communications

Some specializations can be:

- Direct Marketing
- Retail Marketing
- Business to Business Marketing
- Web/Internet Marketing
- Global Marketing

11.1.3 Finance

The functional area of Finance[4] is generally composed of the disciplines of Finance and Accounting, as both have money as their primary language.

As such, Finance is the area of the organization that should be formed mainly by the following two sub-areas:

1. *Treasury* – Management of the organization's financial assets

   - Accounts Payable
   - Accounts Receivable
   - Current Assets Management
     - Cash Flow Management
     - Bank Relationship
     - Financing
     - Investments
     - Other Current Assets

2. *Controllership* – Protection and analysis of use of all assets

   - Accounting
   - Budgeting (if decentralized)
   - External (preparation) & internal (under the Board) Audits
   - Financial Analysis and Reporting
   - Internal Control

A great deal of effort in the Finance area is dedicated to:

- Recording transactions that have financial value
- Managing current assets
- Protecting and analyzing use of the organization's assets

Some basic concepts that are important for all managers to understand, especially as they move up on the organization hierarchy, are:

- Accounts vs. Cost/Result Centers
- Double Entry Accounting
- Cash Basis vs. Accrual Basis
- Income vs. Revenue

- Expense vs. Liability
- Depreciation and Amortization
- Capital Investment
- Cash On Hand vs. Operational Profit/Loss
- Breakeven Point
- Inventory
- Financial Statements
  - Balance Sheet
  - Income Statement / P&L
  - Cash Flow

Balance Sheet

The Balance Sheet is extremely important to understand because it is the broadest report that an organization can produce. It consolidates the performance of all areas, from their creation to the date that the report is generated.

The report has two sides. One side lists the balance of all the assets that the organization was able to acquire and produce throughout its existence. The other side, with equivalent monetary value, lists in two major groups (internal and external agents) that have claim over the assets held by the organization.

For instance, if an organization buys a vehicle and does not pay it in full, the Balance Sheet should record the possession of the vehicle on the assets side of the Balance Sheet, minus money from the bank given as down payment. The other side of the Balance Sheet, under Liabilities (external agents), records the difference not yet paid. The difference to complete the value of the vehicle on the side of the Balance Sheet that reports who has claim over the asset was already recorded under Equity or Net Assets (internal agents – stockholders) when the money for the down payment was first deposited in the bank. This process is called double entry. This means that until the vehicle is completely paid, the seller has some claim on some of the organization's assets equivalent to the amount so far unpaid.

Another important thing to understand is that the result generated in the Income Statement is plugged into the Balance Sheet Earnings account under Equity. In other words, income and expense accounts by themselves do not have balances. It is like counting how much wealth has passed through the organization's door during a certain period. No wealth is left at the door, but there will always be a positive or negative balance left inside the organization. (Note: Negative balance means increased liability.)

Visual representation of the relationship between Balance Sheet and Income Statement

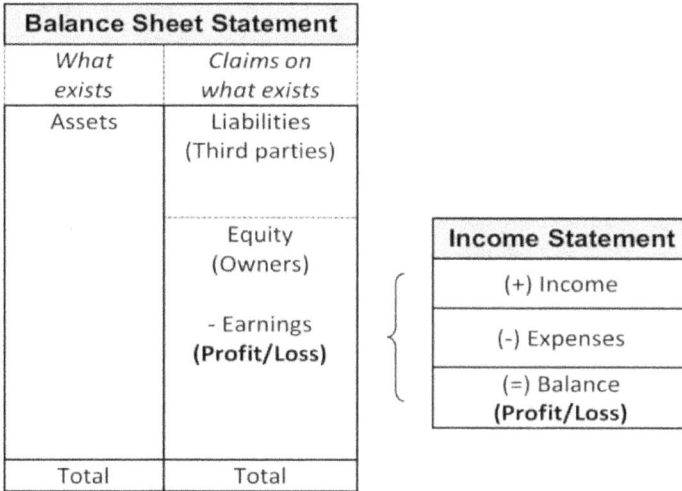

Balance Sheet Statement	
What exists	*Claims on what exists*
Assets	Liabilities (Third parties)
	Equity (Owners)
	- Earnings **(Profit/Loss)**
Total	Total

Income Statement
(+) Income
(-) Expenses
(=) Balance **(Profit/Loss)**

Figure 11.1.3.a

Double Entry

Each transaction should be recorded twice, each representing one side of the same transaction. For example, who has paid and who has received, or how something was paid for and what was received in return.

Effect of double entry on each type of account (increase / decrease account)

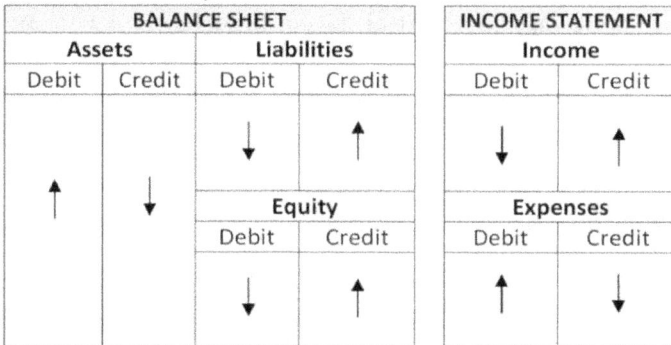

Figure 11.1.3.c

Type of Account	When an entry is recorded as a DEBIT	When an entry is recorded as a CREDIT
Balance Sheet Accounts		
Asset	↑	↓
Liability	↓	↑
Equity	↓	↑
Income Statement Accounts		
Income	↓	↑
Expenses	↑	↓

Figure 11.1.3.b

11.1.4 Human Affairs

Humans are not resources; hence, an appropriate name for this area of specialization will have to come from a deeper understanding of the true relationship between capital and labor.

This being the case, the utmost consideration must be extended to all personnel in an organization. At the same time, all aspects related to personnel should be carried out with extreme care and backed internally and/or externally by professionals specialized in labor laws.

Some of the main concerns of the functional area of Human Affairs[5] should be:

- Job analysis and design
- Organizational fit
- Performance
- Support
- Compensation
- Labor laws

Shaped by each organization's mission, strategy, policies, and bylaws, a Human Affairs "cycle" might be as follows:

1. Job
   1.1. Job analysis
   1.2. Job design and description

2. Staffing
   2.1. Recruiting
   2.2. Selection
   2.3. Hiring
   2.4. Organizational entry and socialization

3. Maintenance
   3.1. Compensation and benefits
   3.2. Labor hygiene and security
   3.3. Maintenance of morale and discipline
   3.4. Labor relations

4. Supporting

5. Monitoring
   5.1. Basic personnel data
   5.2. Performance
   5.3. Analysis and reports
   5.4. Internal audit

6. Development
   6.1. Training
   6.2. Promotion and transfers

7. Dissociation

11.1.5 Information Technology

As the name implies, Information Technology[6] (IT) makes use of technology in order to handle the manipulation (capture, storage, processing, and dissemination) of information and the facilitation of communication, both inside the organization and with external stakeholders.

IT should not be confused with other areas that deal with computer technology, such as the application of robots in a production line.

In order to achieve their objectives, many IT departments focus their attention primarily on the following areas:

- Network – Cables, Wireless, Intranets, Internet
- Hardware – Servers, Workstations, Mobile Devices, Integration with other products
- Operational Systems
- Databases
- Application programs (software)
- Users

A great deal of energy goes into:

- Systems Analysis and Design
- Database Management, Data Mining, Document Management, Content Management
- Technical Support and Maintenance
- Computer and Network Security
- Keeping up with the evolution technology – hardware, software, and so forth

From the user's perspective, application programs are generally more relevant than hardware; especially those programs that help automate work and facilitate business. These programs can be bought as a completed product, developed in-house, or custom-ordered according to specifications. Because the development and maintenance of software developed in-house is often quite a challenge, this practice has become restricted to special cases.

Strategically speaking, two major challenges to IT are:

a. To determine the technology that provides the organization the best cost/benefit ratio.

b. To strike the right balance between the work that should be done in-house and the work that should be outsourced.

For managers dealing with the IT area, the utilization of Project Management and Change Management programs are almost a must, as upgrades and conversions of software and hardware, training, and so forth, are commonplace endeavors.

11.2 Generalist

Although it is possible to say that a person, usually a consultant, has specialized in one management function, the term generalist is never used to refer to someone who has a well-rounded knowledge of the occupation of management. Instead, the term is always used in connection with non-managerial work, even if the generalist is a manager.

Accordingly, the term generalist is commonly used to refer to a person who manages several activities of a functional area like Human Affairs (Resources). Instead of a company staffing the department with different specialists, such as Benefits and Compensation, Recruiting, and Training, it tries to utilize a single person to handle all the different aspects of the area. Likewise, the term can also be applied to top-level managers who are expected to be knowledgeable about multiple non-managerial works areas, as in the case of a vice-president responsible for the functional areas of Finance, Human Affairs, IT, and General Services.

In the final analysis, it might be possible to say that the difference between the description of Generalist and Specialist is one of perspective— that is to say, the distinction depends on the number of areas to which one is referring, regardless of their level in the organizational structure. The only exception is in the Task domain, where one can only be specialist.

Unfortunately, in practice the opportunities for becoming a generalist by moving around different areas is usually limited, as organizations tend to consider the cost/benefit of rotating individuals between different work areas as disadvantageous. Organizations also tend to look at individuals as uncommitted if they become generalists by learning multiple trades through different organizations.

The two most common paths to becoming a generalist are through promotion to a managerial position and through study. The path of study will not be discussed further here. Regarding the path of promotion, however, it is important to note that being a generalist is intrinsic to the concept of management. In the final analysis, it is a requirement of the occupation to facilitate the integration of divided work. Like it or not, by assuming a managerial position, one is automatically exposed to multiple work areas.

The result is that it is relatively common for individuals to take on the responsibility of multiple work areas without having acquired sufficient expertise in all of them. To try to overcome this deficiency at middle and top management levels, individuals are encouraged or required in some cases to take management courses before or after assuming a managerial position. Still, in some organizations with more resources, a quick rotation through different work areas is usually added to the preparation mix of a person selected to assume a top-level managerial position.

Regardless, when this upwards hierarchical movement happens, if managers assume that they should be the experts, they will occasionally find themselves in awkward situations. It is unrealistic to think that managers should know more than their direct reports know in order to avoid losing "face" and credibility. One only loses face and credibility if one insists on making decisions alone despite lacking the knowledge to do so.

The point is that with the amount of knowledge and complexity out there, generalist managers can rarely know more than each one of the "specialists" in all the areas for which they are responsible. Generalists should not expect to reach the level of expertise in multiple areas that one person is capable of achieving as a specialist of a single area. Consequently, managers should be prepared to become more and more dependent on direct reports as they climb the organizational ladder. This fact needs to be accepted by all. This gives managers, and above all top-level managers, one more reason to be humble and consultative in their dealings with their direct reports.

Into a New Era

At a glance, it might seem that *The Science and Spirit of Management* dedicates considerably more attention to the scientific aspect of the discipline than to the spirit that should animate it, but that is not so. Instead of presenting ideals in a format that is difficult to translate into practice, the book describes the practice of management from a perspective that places the discipline in conformity with humans' higher nature and with the true purpose of organizations. The spirit that should exist in management is presented in many instances through the display of its application.

For example, both the definition of management as the endeavor of facilitating the collective production of deliverables and the description of the functions that managers should carry out are imbued with a spirit that reflects the reality of humans as social beings. Such a view is the outcome of a paradigm that acknowledges a manager as one of many interdependent components of an organic system. Consequently, organizations can only reach a state of wholeness when its diverse components fully integrate with each other.

As a result, this paradigm bars dictatorial posture from managers and simultaneously adjusts the emphasis that is presently placed on leaders in the context of the discipline of management. It does not accept the exploitation of some elements for the sake of others, because it assumes that a selfish driving force is misaligned with the very essence of organization and teamwork as a communal undertaking for collective wellbeing. Instead, by accepting the reality of oneness, managers contribute to the process with a spirit of service.

Such an approach to management requires managers to be staunch up-holders of justice and possessors of positive qualities, such as truthfulness, humility and courtesy. In a broader sense, the movement into a new era of management necessitates that human relationships be "re-conceptualized", that we find a fresh, more elevated way of interacting with each other.

> *The second attribute of perfection is justice and impartiality. This means to have no regard for one's own personal benefits and selfish advantages... It means, in brief, to regard humanity as a single individual, and one's own self as a member of that corporeal form, and to know of a certainty that if pain or injury afflicts any member of that body, it must inevitably result in suffering for all the rest.[1]*
>
> 'Abdu'l-Bahá,

> *That one indeed is a man who, today, dedicateth himself to the service of the entire human race.[2]*
>
> Bahá'u'lláh

Notes

Many of the topics in this book are presented in an innovative way, as far as the author knows. Consequently, most of the references are intended to serve primarily as examples of other works for complementary or alternative purposes.

Introduction

1. For *Classical School*, see for example Fayol, Henri. *General and Industrial Management*. Translated from the French Edition (Dunod) by Constance Storrs. Martino Publishing, 2013. Print.

   See also Thompson, Clarence B. – Editor. *Scientific Management: A Collection of the Most Significant Articles Describing the Taylor System of Management*. Harvard Business Press, 1914.
   http://archive.org/details/scientificmanage00thomuoft

   See also Urwick, L. *The Function of Administration – With Special Reference to the Work of Henri Fayol*. A Lecture Delivered Before the Institute of Industrial Administration, 13th November 1934. In: Papers on the Science of Administration. Institute of Public Administration. The Rumford Press. 1937.
   http://archive.org/stream/papersonscienceo00guli/papersonscienceo00guli_djvu.txt

2. Regarding clarity of definitions, see also foreword by Urwick, L. to Henri Fayol's General and Industrial Management. Translated from the French Edition (Dunod) by Constance Storrs. Martino Publishing, 2013. Print.

3. Bahá'í International Community. *Rethinking Prosperity: Forging Alternatives to a Culture of Consumerism*. Contribution to the 18th Session of the United Nations Commission on Sustainable Development. http://www.bic.org/statements/rethinking-prosperity-forging-alternatives-culture-consumerism

Chapter 1

1. See 'Abdu'l-Bahá. *Some Answered Questions* (48: The Difference Existing Between Man and Animal). Collected and Translated by Laura

Clifford Barney. Wilmette, IL: Bahá'í Publishing Trust, 1987. Print. Digital: http://reference.bahai.org/en/t/ab/SAQ/

2. Ibid., (36: The Five Aspects of Spirit).

3. See 'Abdu'l-Bahá. *Tablet to August Forel.* Original Persian text first published Cairo 1922. This translation taken from The Bahá'í World, Vol. XV, pg. 37-43. George Ronald Publishers, 1978. Digital: http://reference.bahai.org/en/t/ab/TAF/)

Chapter 2

1. Mooney, James D. *The Principles of Organization.* Both In: Papers on the Science of Administration. Institute of Public Administration. The Rumford Press, 1937. http://archive.org/stream/papersonscienceo00guli/papersonscienceo00guli_djvu.txt

2. For *Subordination of Individual Interest to General Interest,* see Fayol, Henri. *General and Industrial Management.* Translated from the French Edition (Dunod) by Constance Storrs. Martino Publishing, 2013. Print.

3. Bahá'í International Community. *The Prosperity of Humankind.* 1995. Statement Library. http://statements.bahai.org/95-0303.htm

4. Ibid.

5. For *Core Competence,* see Prahalad, C. K. and Hamel, Gary. *The Core Competence of the Corporation.* Harvard Business Review, (v. 68, no. 3), pg. 79–91, 1990. http://hbr.org/

   See also Treacy, Michael and Wiersema, Fred. *The Discipline of Market Leaders.* Reading, MA: Addison-Wesley, 1995. Print.

6. For *Organizational Life Cycle,* see also Scott. In: Steiner, G.A. and Miner, J.B.. *Política e Estratégia Administrativa.* Rio de Janeiro: Interciência/São Paulo: Edusp, 1981. Reprinted in Cury, Antonio. *Organização e Métodos: Uma Visão Holística.* 7ª Edição. Editora Atlas, 2000. Print.

7. For *Formal and Informal "Organization"* see also Selfridge, R.J. & Sokolick, S.L.. *A Comprehensive View of Organizational Development.*

MSU Business Topics, 47, 1975. Cited in Stroh, Linda; Northcraft, Gregory; Neale, Margaret. *Organizational Behavior: A Management Challenge.* 3ª Edição: Lawrence Erlbaum Associates, Publishers, 2002. Print.

8. For *informal sphere*, see also Roethlisberger and Dickson cited by Henderson, L. J.; Whitehead, T. N. and Mayo, Elton. *The Effects of Social Environment.* Graduate School of Business Administration, Harvard University. In: Papers on the Science of Administration. Institute of Public Administration. The Rumford Press. 1937.
http://archive.org/stream/papersonscienceo00guli/papersonscienceo00g uli_djvu.txt

9. For *Open System and Holistic View*, see also Follett, Mary Parker. *The Process of Control.* The final lecture in a series delivered at the London School of Economics in 1932. In: Papers on the Science of Administration. Institute of Public Administration. The Rumford Press. 1937.
http://archive.org/stream/papersonscienceo00guli/papersonscienceo00g uli_djvu.txt

For *Open System*, see also Cury, Antonio. *Organização e Métodos: Uma Visão Holística.* 7ª Edição: Editora Atlas, 2000, reprinting work of Lawrence, P. R. and Lorsch, J. W.. *As Empresas e o Ambiente.* Petrópolis: Vozes, 1973, (based on Burns, T. and Stalker, G. M.. *The Management of Innovation.*). Print.

10. For *Holist View*, see also Cury, Antonio. *Organização e Métodos: Uma Visão Holística.* 7ª Edição: Editora Atlas, 2000, pg. 122-3. Citing Steiner, G.A. and Miner, J.B. *Política e Estratégia Administrativa.* Rio de Janeiro: Interciência/São Paulo: Edusp, 1981, pg. 46-47 and Thompson, J. D. *Dinâmica Organizacional.* São Paulo, McGraw-Hill do Brasil, 1976, pg. 20, 26-7.

See also the work of Talcott Parsons and Niklas Luhmann related to "Social System".

11. For *Departmentalization,* see also Gulick, L.. *Notes on the Theory of Organization.* In: Papers on the Science of Administration. Institute of Public Administration. The Rumford Press, 1937.
http://archive.org/stream/papersonscienceo00guli/papersonscienceo00g uli_djvu.txt

See also Urwick, L. *Organization as a Technical Problem*. Paper II of this collection; Frederick A. Cleveland, "Expert Staff Aids to Management," Industrial Service and Equipment Co., Boston, 1918; James D. Mooney and Alan C. Reiley, "Onward Industry!" Harper and Brothers, New York, 1931.

See also Cury, Antonio. *Organização e Métodos: Uma Visão Holística*. 7ª Edição: Editora Atlas, 2000. Print.

12. For *Organizational Structure*, see also Cury, Antonio. *Organização e Métodos: Uma Visão Holística*. 7ª Edição: Editora Atlas, 2000. Print.

For a discussion of "Functional Structure" only, see also Lee, John. *The Pros and Cons of Functionalization*, from the report of the twenty-seventh lecture conference for works directors, managers, foremen and forewomen, held at Balliol College, Oxford, September 27th to 30th, 1928. In: Papers on the Science of Administration. Institute of Public Administration. The Rumford Press, 1937.
http://archive.org/stream/papersonscienceo00guli/papersonscienceo00guli_djvu.txt

13. The concept that "structure follows strategy" is attributed to Alfred Chandler. See Chandler, A.D. Jr.. *Strategy and Structure: Chapters in the History of the American Industrial Enterprise*. Cambridge, MA: MIT Press, 1990. Print.

Chapter 3

1. For *Interpersonal*, see also Schein, Edgar H.. *Process Consultation Revisited: Building the Helping Relationship*. Addison-Wesley Series on Organization Development, 1999.

See also Reddy, W. Brendan. *Intervention Skills: Process of Consultation for Small Groups and Teams*. 1st Edition. Jossey-Bass/Pfeiffer, 1994. Print.

For *Direct and Indirect Contact* ("written and verbal communication"), see *Espirit the Corps* in Fayol, Henri. *General and Industrial Management*. Translated from the French Edition (Dunod) by Constance Storrs. Martino Publishing, 2013. Print.

2. For *Work Groups* (for a difference between Work Groups and Teams), see also Brounstein, Marty. Managing Teams for Dummies. Wiley, 2002. Print. E-Book.

3. For *Teams*, see also Reddy, W. Brendan. *Team Building: Blueprints for Productivity and Satisfaction*. NTL Institute for Applied Behavioral Science, 1988. Print.

   See also Dyer, William G.. *Team Building: Current Issues and New Alternatives*. Addison-Wesley Publishing, 1995. Print.

4. For *Task*, see also Cury, Antonio. *Organização e Métodos: Uma Visão Holística*. 7ª Edição: Editora Atlas, 2000. Print.

5. Honda Corporation's principle – Cited in Lawrence M. Mille' blog: http://www.lmmiller.com/blog/2013/02/18/corporate-culture/joy-at-work-happiness-and-performance-what-we-know-and-what-you-should-do/

6. For *Activity*, see also Cury, Antonio. *Organização e Métodos: Uma Visão Holística*. 7ª Edição. Editora Atlas, 2000. Print.

7. For *Functional Area* ("Function"), see also Cury, Antonio. *Organização e Métodos: Uma Visão Holística*. 7ª Edição. Editora Atlas, 2000. Print.

8. For *Geographical* ("Geographic"), see also Gulick, L. *Notes on the Theory of Organization*. In: Papers on the Science of Administration. Institute of Public Administration. The Rumford Press, 1937. http://archive.org/stream/papersonscienceo00guli/papersonscienceo00g uli_djvu.txt

9. For *Virtual* work ("Telework", "Remote Work", "Telecommuting"), see also Amigoni, Michael and Gurvis, Sandra. *Managing the Telecommuting Employee: Set Goals, Monitor Progress, Maximize Profits and Productivity*. Adams Business, 2009. Print.

10. For *Outsourcing*, see also Power, Mark J.; Desouza, Kevin C.; Bonifazi, Carlo. *The Outsourcing Handbook: How to Implement a Successful Outsourcing Process*. 1st Edition. Kogan Page Limited, 2006. Print.

11. For *Process*, see also Cruz, Tadeu. *Sistemas, Métodos & Processos: Administrando Organizações por meio de Processos de Negócios*. Editora Atlas, 2002. Print.

See also Cury, Antonio. *Organização e Métodos: Uma Visão Holística.* 7ª Edição. Editora Atlas, 2000. Print.

12. For a more detailed explanation of *Flowcharts,* see Cury, Antonio. *Organização e Métodos: Uma Visão Holística.* 7ª Edição. Editora Atlas, 2000. Print.

13. For a more detailed explanation of *Forms,* see Cury, A. *Organização e Métodos: Uma Visão Holística.* 7ª Edição. Editora Atlas, 2000. Print.

14. For *Management levels,* see also See also Urwick, L. *Organization as a Technical Problem.* Based on a paper read to the department of industrial co-operation of the British Association for the Advancement of Science, Leicester, September j, 1933. In: Papers on the Science of Administration. Institute of Public Administration. The Rumford Press, 1937. http://archive.org/stream/papersonscienceo00guli/papersonscienceo00g uli_djvu.txt

See also Cury, Antonio. *Organização e Métodos: Uma Visão Holística.* 7ª Edição. Editora Atlas, 2000. Print.

Chapter 4

1. For *Division of Labor,* see also Gulick, L. *Notes on the Theory of Organization.* In: Papers on the Science of Administration. Institute of Public Administration. The Rumford Press, 1937. http://archive.org/stream/papersonscienceo00guli/papersonscienceo00g uli_djvu.txt

2. For *Management Functions,* see also Fayol, Henri. *General and Industrial Management.* Translated from the French Edition (Dunod) by Constance Storrs. Martino Publishing, 2013. Print.

3. For *Leadership,* see also Bahá'u'lláh, Abdu'l-Bahá, Shoghi Effendi, and Universal House of Justice. *Unlocking the Power of Action.* Complied by Research Department of the Universal House of Justice. Digital: http://bahai-library.com/compilation_unlocking_power_action

   See also Barnard, Chester I. *The Functions of the Executive.* 30th Anniversary Edition. Harvard University Press, 1971. Print.

4. For *"Lust of Leadership",* see Bahá'u'lláh. *The Kitáb-i-Íqán.* Translated by Shoghi Effendi. Wilmette, IL: Bahá'í Publishing Trust, 1983. Print.

Digital: http://reference.bahai.org/en/t/b/KI/

5. From a letter dated 17 February 1933 written on behalf of Shoghi Effendi, published in *Conservation of the Earth's Resources*, Comp. Research Department of the Universal House of Justice. (Mona Vale: National Spiritual Assembly of the Bahá'ís of Australia, 1989), pg.21-22.

6. Bahá'u'lláh. *The Hidden Words*. Wilmette, IL: Bahá'í Publishing Trust, 1994. Print. Digital: http://reference.bahai.org/en/t/b/HW/

7. 'Abdu'l-Bahá. *Paris Talks*. London: Bahá'í Publishing Trust, 1995, pg. 152. Print. Digital: http://reference.bahai.org/en/t/ab/PT/

8. For *Authority, see also "Authority and Responsibility", "Unity of Command", and "Unity of Direction" in* Fayol, Henri. *General and Industrial Management*. Translated from the French Edition (Dunod) by Constance Storrs. Martino Publishing, 2013. Print.

9. Bahá'u'lláh. *The Kitáb-i-Aqdas*. Haifa, Israel: Bahá'í World Centre, 1992. Print. Digital: http://reference.bahai.org/en/t/b/KA/

10. For *Analysis, s*ee also Sanvicente, Antonio Z. *Administração Financeira*. 3ª Edição. Editora Atlas, 1987. Print.

11. For *Diagnosis, s*ee also Cummings & Worley. *Organization Development & Change*. 7th Edition. South-Western College – Thomson Learning, 2001. Print.

12. For *Causes*, see also 'Abdu'l-Bahá. *Some Answered Questions* (80: Real Preexistence). Collected and Translated by Laura Clifford Barney. Wilmette, IL: Bahá'í Publishing Trust: 1987, pg. 279. Print. Digital: http://reference.bahai.org/en/t/ab/SAQ/

13. For *Planning*, see also Fayol, Henri. *General and Industrial Management*. Translated from the French Edition (Dunod) by Constance Storrs. Martino Publishing, 2013. Print.

14. For *Mission*, see also Romig, Dennis A.. *Breakthrough Teamwork: Outstanding Results Using Structured Teamwork*. Romig. Performance Research Press, 1996. Print.

15. For *Visions*, see also Romig, Dennis A.. *Breakthrough Teamwork: Outstanding Results Using Structured Teamwork*. Romig. Performance Research Press, 1996. Print.

16. The origin of the SMART acronyms does not seem to be clear. See Morrison, Mike. http://rapidbi.com/history-of-smart-objectives/. However, many attribute its creation to Doran, George; Miller, Arthur; Cunningham, James. *There's an S.M.A.R.T. way to write management's goals and objectives*. Management Review 1981, vol. 70, issue 11, pg. 35-6.

    For *Management by Objectives*, see Peter Drucker.

17. For *Policies*, see also Cury, Antonio. *Organização e Métodos: Uma Visão Holística*. 7ª Edição. Editora Atlas, 2000. Print.

18. For *Organizing*, see also in Fayol, Henri. *General and Industrial Management*. Translated from the French Edition (Dunod) by Constance Storrs. Martino Publishing, 2013. Print.

    See also Gulick, L. *Notes on the Theory of Organization*. See also Mooney, James D. *The Principles of Organization*. Both In: Papers on the Science of Administration. Institute of Public Administration. The Rumford Press, 1937.
    http://archive.org/stream/papersonscienceo00guli/papersonscienceo00g uli_djvu.txt

    See also Cury, Antonio. *Organização e Métodos: Uma Visão Holística*. 7ª Edição. Editora Atlas, 2000. Print.

19. For *Coordinating*, see also Urwick, L. *Organization as a Technical Problem*. Based on a paper read to the department of industrial co-operation of the British Association for the Advancement of Science, Leicester, September j, 1933. See also Follett, Mary Parker. *The Process of Control*. The final lecture in a series delivered at the London School of Economics in 1932. Both in: Papers on the Science of Administration. Institute of Public Administration. The Rumford Press, 1937.
    http://archive.org/stream/papersonscienceo00guli/papersonscienceo00g uli_djvu.txt

20. For *Monitoring*, see also "Control" in Fayol, Henri. *General and Industrial Management*. Translated from the French Edition (Dunod) by Constance Storrs. Martino Publishing, 2013. Print.

21. For *Performance Review (Appraisal)*, see also Performance Appraisal. Wikipedia, The free Encyclopedia.

http://en.wikipedia.org/wiki/Performance_appraisal

See also Bersin, J. *Time to Scrap Performance Appraisals?* Forbes.com, 2013.
http://www.forbes.com/sites/joshbersin/2013/05/06/time-to-scrap-performance-appraisals/

22. For *Supporting* ("Empowerment" only), see also Bahá'í International Community. *Empowerment as a Mechanism for Social Transformation.* Contribution to the 51st Session of the Commission for Social Development. 15 November 2012, New York.
http://www.bic.org/statements/empowerment-mechanism-social-transformation

For "Empowerment" only, see also Romig, Dennis A.. *Breakthrough Teamwork: Outstanding Results Using Structured Teamwork.* Romig. Performance Research Press, 1996. Print.

23. For *Cultural Modeling,* see also "Subordination of Individual Interest to General Interest" in Fayol, Henri. *General and Industrial Management.* Translated from the French Edition (Dunod) by Constance Storrs. Martino Publishing, 2013. Print.

Chapter 5

1. For *Span of Direct Management* ("Span of Control"), see also V. A. Graicunas, *Relationship in Organization.* See also Gulick, L. *Notes on the Theory of Organization.* See also Urwick, L. *Organization as a Technical Problem.* All in: Papers on the Science of Administration. Institute of Public Administration. The Rumford Press, 1937.
http://archive.org/stream/papersonscienceo00guli/papersonscienceo00guli_djvu.txt

2. For what is perhaps the most popular Team Life Cycle model, see Tuckman, Bruce. *Developmental Sequence in Small Groups.* The American Psychological Association, Psychological Bulletin, 1965, V. 63, N. 6, pgs 384–99. He later improved his model in partnership with Jensen, M.A. (1977). The team life cycle model presented by Truckman and Jensen has persisted, with only small variations made by different scholars and practitioners. In this book, the two main differences are the approach to the Forming stage and the elimination of the Storming

stage. The idea is that potential team members should be better prepared to join teams, and teams should formally tackle Norming right from the start. (Storming = phase where team members start to operate together without basic rules and where members begin to accommodate each other.)

3. For *team-related issues*, see also Miller, Lawrence M. *The Team Guide to Continuous Improvement.* Miller Management Press, 2012. Print.

See also Romig, Dennis A.. *Breakthrough Teamwork: Outstanding Results Using Structured Teamwork.* Romig. Performance Research Press, 1996. Print.

See also, Katzenbach, Jon R. and Smith, Douglas K.. *The Wisdom of Teams: Creating the High-Performance Organization.* McKinsey & Company, Inc., 1999. Print.

See also, Heller, Robert. *Essential Managers: Managing Teams.* DK Publishing, 1999. Print.

4. For *Delegation*, see also Mooney, James D. *The Principles of Organization.* In: Papers on the Science of Administration. Institute of Public Administration. The Rumford Press, 1937.
http://archive.org/stream/papersonscienceo00guli/papersonscienceo00guli_djvu.txt

For *Decentralization and Delegation*, see also Cury, Antonio. *Organização e Métodos: Uma Visão Holística.* 7ª Edição. Editora Atlas, 2000. Print.

5. For *Decentralization and "Centralization"*, see also Fayol, Henri. *General and Industrial Management.* Translated from the French Edition (Dunod) by Constance Storrs. Martino Publishing, 2013. Print.

Chapter 6

1. For *Manager's Personal Qualities*, see also 'Abdu'l-Bahá. *The Secret of Divine Civilization.* Wilmette, IL: Bahá'í Publishing Trust, 1990, Print. Digital: http://reference.bahai.org/en/t/ab/SDC/

See also Marcic, Dorothy. *Managing with the Wisdom of Love: Uncovering Virtue in People and Organizations.* 1st Edition. Jossey-Bass, 1997. Print.

2. For *Self-mastery* ("Personal Mastery"), see also Senge, Peter M. *The Fifth Discipline: The Art and Practice of the Learning Organization.* Doubleday, 1990. Print.

3. 'Abdu'l-Bahá, cited in *Lights of Guidance: A Bahá'í Reference File.* Compiled by Helen Bassett Hornby. New Delhi, India: Bahá'í Publishing Trust, 1994, pg. 114. Print. Digital format can be downloaded from http://bahai-education.org/ocean/

4. From a letter written on behalf of Shoghi Effendi to an individual believer, December 10, 1947. *Lights of Guidance*, pg. 113. Print. Digital format can be downloaded from http://bahai-education.org/ocean/

5. Bahá'u'lláh. *Gleanings from the Writings of Bahá'u'lláh.* Wilmette, IL: Bahá'í Publishing Trust, 1983, pg. 93. Print.
Digital: http://reference.bahai.org/en/t/b/GWB/

6. For *Golden Rule*, see Wikipedia:
http://en.wikipedia.org/wiki/Golden_Rule

7. Bahá'u'lláh. *Epistle to the Son of the Wolf.* Wilmette, IL: Bahá'í Publishing Trust, 1988, pg. 29. Print.
Digital: http://reference.bahai.org/en/t/b/ESW/

For *People Skills*, see also Luft, Joseph. *Group Process: An Introduction to Group Dynamics.* Joseph Luft, 1984. Print.

8. Bahá'u'lláh. *Tablets of Bahá'u'lláh.* Wilmette, IL: Bahá'í Publishing Trust, 1988, pg. 66. Print. Digital ("Tablets of Bahá'u'lláh Revealed After the Kitáb-i-Aqdas"): http://reference.bahai.org/en/t/b/TB/

9. For *Distributive*, *Procedural* and *Interactive* justice, see also Stroh, Linda; Northcraft, Gregory; Neale, Margaret. *Organizational Behavior: A Management Challenge.* 3ª Edition. Lawrence Erlbaum Associates, Publishers, 2002. Print.

See also Equity theory – Adams, J. S.. *Toward and Understanding of Inequity.* Journal of Abnormal and Social Psychology, 1963, 67, 422-436. https://apa.org/

10. Bahá'í International Community (1995). *The Prosperity of Humankind.* Statement Library – http://statements.bahai.org/95-0303.htm

11. Ibid.

12. For *Groupthink,* see also http://en.wikipedia.org/wiki/Groupthink. As the article explains, the term "groupthink" was coined by Whyte, William H., Jr.. *Groupthink.* Fortune magazine, March 1952, pg. 114.

13. 'Abdu'l-Bahá. *Selections from the Writings of 'Abdu'l-Bahá.* Haifa, Israel: Bahá'í World Centre, 1982, pg. 87. Print.
    Digital: http://reference.bahai.org/en/t/ab/SAB/

14. Bahá'u'lláh. *Tablets of Bahá'u'lláh.* Wilmette, IL: Bahá'í Publishing Trust, 1988, pg. 72. Print. Digital ("Tablets of Bahá'u'lláh Revealed After the Kitáb-i-Aqdas"):
    http://reference.bahai.org/en/t/b/TB/

15. For the concept that "structure drives behavior", see also Mooney, James D. *The Principles of Organization.* In: Papers on the Science of Administration. Institute of Public Administration. The Rumford Press, 1937.
    http://archive.org/stream/papersonscienceo00guli/papersonscienceo00guli_djvu.txt

16. See 'Abdu'l-Bahá. *Tablet to August Forel.* Original Persian text first published Cairo 1922. This translation taken from The Bahá'í World, Vol. XV, pg. 37-43. George Ronald Publishers, 1978. Digital: http://reference.bahai.org/en/t/ab/TAF/

    See also, Bahá'u'lláh. *The Summons of the Lord of Hosts.* Bahá'í World Centre, 2002 edition, pg. 154-5: gr35.
    Digital: http://reference.bahai.org/en/t/b/SLH/

17. 'Abdu'l-Bahá. *Paris Talks* (Address by 'Abdu'l-Bahá at the Friends' Meeting House, St Martin's Lane, London, W.C.). London: Bahá'í Publishing Trust, 1995, pg. 174. Print.
    Digital: http://reference.bahai.org/en/t/ab/PT/

18. For the concept of "Knowing-Doing Gap", see also Pfeffer, Jeffrey and Sutton, Robert I.. *The Knowing-Doing Gap: How Smart Companies Turn Knowledge Into Action.* Harvard Business School Press, 2000. Print.

Chapter 7

1. "Bahá'u'lláh says there is a sign (from God) in every phenomenon: the sign of the intellect is contemplation and the sign of contemplation is

silence, because it is impossible for a man to do two things at one time -
- he cannot both speak and meditate." Cited by 'Abdu'l-Bahá. *Paris
Talks* (Address by 'Abdu'l-Bahá at the Friends' Meeting House, St Martin's Lane, London, W.C.). London: Bahá'í Publishing Trust, 1995, pg.
174. Print. Digital: http://reference.bahai.org/en/t/ab/PT/

Chapter 8

1. See Bahá'í International Community. *Protection of Minorities*. United
   States Office, 1990.
   http://www.bic.org/statements/protection-minorities-2

Chapter 9

1. For *Management Tools,* see also Fayol, H. *The Administrative Theory in
   the State.* Address Before the Second International Congress of Administrative Science at Brussels, September 13, 1923. In: Papers on the Science of Administration. Institute of Public Administration. The Rumford Press, 1937.
   http://archive.org/stream/papersonscienceo00guli/papersonscienceo00g
   uli_djvu.txt

2. For *Meetings,* see also Justice, Thomas and Jamilson, David   W.. *The
   Facilitator's Fieldbook.* HRD Press, 1999. Print.

   See also Romig, Dennis A.. *Breakthrough Teamwork: Outstanding Results Using Structured Teamwork.* Romig. Performance Research Press,
   1996. Print.

3. For a more detailed explanation of *Manuals,* see also Cury, Antonio.
   Organização e Métodos: Uma Visão Holística. 7ª Edição. Editora Atlas,
   2000. Print.

4. Bahá'u'lláh. *The Kitáb-i-Aqdas.* Haifa, Israel: Bahá'í World Centre,
   1992. Print. Digital: http://reference.bahai.org/en/t/b/KA/

5. For *Presentations,* see also Rotondo, Jennifer and Rotondo Jr.,
   Mike.*Presentation Skills for Managers.* 1st Edition. McGraw-Hill, 2001.
   Print.

   See also Theobald, Theo. *Develop Your Presentation Skills: Creating Success.* 1st Edition. Kogan Page, 2011. Print.

6. For *Other Management Tools*, see the Web.

Chapter 10

1. For *Strategic Management*, see also Wheelen, Thomas L. and Hunger, J. David. *Strategic Management and Business Policy*. 8th Edition. Prentice Hall, 2002. Print.

2. For earlier work on *SWOT Analysis*, see Selznick, Philip; Humphrey, Albert; Learned, Edmund P.; Kenneth R. Andrews, and others. Harvard Business School.

3. For *Directional Strategies*, see also Wheelen, Thomas L. and Hunger, J. David. *Strategic Management and Business Policy*. 8th Edition. Prentice Hall, 2002. Print.

4. For *Business Unit Portfolio/Compatibility Strategies* ("Parenting-fit"), see Campbell, Andrew, Michael Goold and Marcus Alexander. *Corporate Strategy: The Quest for Parenting Advantage*. Harvard Business Review, 1995. http://hbr.org/ (*Parenting-fit* denotes classes of compatibility between business units and the parent organization, and consequently between a business unit with the corporation in its entirety.)

5. For *Product Portfolio Strategies*, see the *BCG* (Boston Consulting Group) *Matrix* developed by Bruce Henderson. The model analyzes an organization's product portfolio based on market share, potential for market growth, and positive or negative cash flow. http://www.bcg.com/about_bcg/history/history_1968.aspx

6. For *Competitive Strategies,* see M. E. Porter. *Competitive Advantage: Techniques for Analyzing Industries and Competitors*. 1st Edition. The Free Press, 1980. Print.

7. For *Budget Management,* see also Bragg, Steven M.. *Budgeting: A Comprehensive Guide*. Steven M. Bragg, Centennial, Colorado, 2011. Print.

   See also Brookson, Stephen. *Essential Managers: Managing Budgets*. DK Publishing, 2000. Print.

8. For *Change Management*, see also Cummings & Worley. *Organization Development & Change*. 7th Edition. South-Western College – Thomson Learning, 2001. Print.

See also Taylor, Frederick W. (1911). *Shop Management.* The Project Gutenberg EBook. Transcribed by Charles E. Nichols. Release Date: September, 2004 [EBook #6464] - http://gutenberg.net

9. See Lewin, K. (1947). *Frontiers in Group Dynamics: Concept, Method and Reality in Social Science, Social Equilibria and Social Change.* Sage Publications, Journals Human Relations. Digital. http://hum.sagepub.com/content/1/1/5.full.pdf+html

10. For *Project Management*, see also Nicholas, John M. *Project Management for Business and Technology: Principles and Practice.* 2nd Edition. Prentice Hall, 2001. Print.

Chapter 11

1. For *Operations,* see also Reid, R. Ran; Sander, Nada R.. *Operations Management: An Integrated Approach.* 3rd Edition. Wiley, 2009. Print.

2. For *Marketing,* see Iacobucci, Dawn – Editor. *Kellogg on Marketing.* The Kellogg Marketing Faculty, Northwestern University. Wiley, 2001. Print.

3. For *Marketing Mix Variables*, see Kotler, Phil. *Marketing Management: Analysis, Planning, and Control.* 4th Edition. Prentice-Hall, 1980. Print.

4. For *Finance,* see also Sanvicente, Antonio Z. *Administração Financeira.* 3ª Edição. Editora Atlas, 1987. Print.

   See also Eisen, Peter J.. *Accounting.* Barron's Educational Series, 1994. Print.

5. For *Human Affairs* ("Human Resources"), see also Chiavenato, Idalberto. *Recursos Humanos.* Edição Compacta. 7ª Edição. Editora Atlas, 2002. Print.

6. For *Information Technology*, see also The Joint Task Force for Computing Curricula. *Computing Curricula 2005: The Overview Report.* A cooperative project of The Association for Computing Machinery (ACM), The Association for Information Systems (AIS) and The Computer Society (IEEE-CS). A volume of the Computing Curricula Series. ACM/IEEE, 2005.
   http://www.acm.org/education/curric_vols/CC2005-March06Final.pdf

See also Schiesser, Rich. *IT Systems Management.* 2nd Edition. Prentice-Hall, 2010. Print.

Into a New Era

1. 'Abdu'l-Bahá, *The Secret of Divine Civilization.* Wilmette, IL: Bahá'í Publishing Trust, 1990, Print.
    Digital: http://reference.bahai.org/en/t/ab/SDC/

2. Bahá'u'lláh. *Tablets of Bahá'u'lláh.* Wilmette, IL. Bahá'í Publishing Trust, 1988, p. 167. Print. Digital ("Tablets of Bahá'u'lláh Revealed After the Kitáb-i-Aqdas"): http://reference.bahai.org/en/t/b/TB/)

About the Author

André Faizi Alves has a Master's Degree in Organization Development from the Graduate School of Business at Loyola University Chicago (USA), and a Bachelor's Degree in Economic Sciences from UNISINOS – Universidade do Vale do Rio dos Sinos (Brazil). He was an associate professor of Organization & Systems and Administrative Methods & Processes at UnB – Universidade de Brasilia (Brazil). His career has highlighted work with Decision Making and Team Management, Organization Development and Change, Strategic Management, and Corporate Finance. He also possesses good general knowledge in most other major functional areas.

Mr. Alves has lived and worked on three different continents, in both government and private sectors, not-for-profit and for-profit organizations, and in production and service industries. His accomplishments include initiating and orchestrating turnarounds, participating in a very successful startup, and contributing toward the advancement of strategies, operations, and cultures in diverse organizations. His professional experience also extends to consulting and training.

The driving force behind all those endeavors is Mr. Alves' constant dedication to serving society. This dedication has also led him to work for many years as a volunteer. In all instances, professional and non-professional, he has focused his heart, mind and actions on making this world a better place. In the process of continuing to contribute to this aim, he now offers this book – *The Science and Spirit of Management* –as a way of assisting with the key issue of management. The hope is that this book will add to managers' capacity to contribute their share in creating better and happier workplaces and, consequently, prosperous organizations for all.

www.ingramcontent.com/pod-product-compliance
Lightning Source LLC
Chambersburg PA
CBHW061201220326
41599CB00025B/4560